Fortifying the Future

Shaila Rana • Rhonda Chicone

Fortifying the Future

Harnessing AI for Transformative Cybersecurity Training

Shaila Rana
ACT Research Institute
San Jose, CA, USA

Rhonda Chicone
ACT Research Institute
San Jose, CA, USA

ISBN 978-3-031-81779-3   ISBN 978-3-031-81780-9 (eBook)
https://doi.org/10.1007/978-3-031-81780-9

© The Editor(s) (if applicable) and The Author(s), under exclusive license to Springer Nature Switzerland AG 2025

This work is subject to copyright. All rights are solely and exclusively licensed by the Publisher, whether the whole or part of the material is concerned, specifically the rights of translation, reprinting, reuse of illustrations, recitation, broadcasting, reproduction on microfilms or in any other physical way, and transmission or information storage and retrieval, electronic adaptation, computer software, or by similar or dissimilar methodology now known or hereafter developed.

The use of general descriptive names, registered names, trademarks, service marks, etc. in this publication does not imply, even in the absence of a specific statement, that such names are exempt from the relevant protective laws and regulations and therefore free for general use.

The publisher, the authors and the editors are safe to assume that the advice and information in this book are believed to be true and accurate at the date of publication. Neither the publisher nor the authors or the editors give a warranty, expressed or implied, with respect to the material contained herein or for any errors or omissions that may have been made. The publisher remains neutral with regard to jurisdictional claims in published maps and institutional affiliations.

This Springer imprint is published by the registered company Springer Nature Switzerland AG
The registered company address is: Gewerbestrasse 11, 6330 Cham, Switzerland

If disposing of this product, please recycle the paper.

Preface

In an era where cyber threats evolve at an unprecedented pace, the need for effective cybersecurity training has never been more critical. As organizations grapple with increasingly sophisticated attacks and a widening cybersecurity skills gap, artificial intelligence emerges as a transformative force in how we prepare our digital defenders.

We began this project with a simple question: How can we leverage artificial intelligence to create more effective, engaging, and adaptive cybersecurity training? As we delved deeper into our research and worked with organizations of various sizes, we discovered that the answer was far more transformative than we initially imagined. AI isn't just an enhancement to existing training methods—it represents a fundamental shift in how we can prepare professionals to defend against cyber threats. We hope you enjoy this book and gain some valuable insights from it to prepare for the wild cybersecurity ride that we are all on.

San Jose, CA, USA	Shaila Rana
San Jose, CA, USA	Rhonda Chicone

Contents

1	**Introduction to AI in Cybersecurity Training**		1
	1.1 The Evolving Landscape of Cyber Threats		2
	1.2 The Importance of Effective Cybersecurity Training		4
		1.2.1 Building a Resilient and Vigilant Workforce	4
		1.2.2 Reducing the Risk and Impact of Cyber Incidents	5
	1.3 The Role of AI in Transforming Cybersecurity Training		6
		1.3.1 Adaptive and Personalized Learning Experiences	9
		1.3.2 Immersive and Engaging Training Environments	12
		1.3.3 Continuous Improvement and Relevance	17
		1.3.4 Generative AI in Cybersecurity Training	20
	1.4 Conclusion of This Chapter		23
	References		23
2	**AI-Driven Personalized Learning in Cybersecurity Training**		25
	2.1 The Benefits of Personalized Learning in Cybersecurity Training		26
		2.1.1 Addressing Individual Knowledge Gaps and Skill Deficiencies	27
		2.1.2 Enhancing Learner Engagement and Retention	30
		2.1.3 Leveraging Learning Techniques	35
	2.2 Implementing AI-Driven Personalized Learning		38
		2.2.1 Defining Goals and Objectives	39
		2.2.2 Creating a Roadmap for Different Organizations	39
		2.2.3 Making It Actionable	40
		2.2.4 Implementation for Individual Learners	40
		2.2.5 Assessing Learner Profiles and Competencies	41
		2.2.6 Designing Adaptive Learning Paths and Content	42
		2.2.7 Monitoring and Optimizing Learning Outcomes	46
	References		50

3 Gamification and Immersive Learning with AI 51
3.1 The Power of Gamification in Cybersecurity Training 52
3.1.1 Increasing Learner Motivation and Engagement 52
3.1.2 Promoting Active Learning and Skill Acquisition 58
3.2 AI-Powered Immersive Learning Experiences 63
3.2.1 Realistic Threat Scenarios and Simulations 63
3.2.2 Virtual Reality and Augmented Reality Applications 68
3.2.3 Balancing Educational Value and Entertainment 70
References 74

4 AI-Generated Realistic Threat Scenarios 77
4.1 The Importance of Realistic Threat Scenarios in Training 77
4.1.1 Exposing Learners to Authentic Cybersecurity Situations 78
4.1.2 Developing Practical Skills and Decision-Making Abilities 79
4.2 AI-Driven Threat Scenario Generation 80
4.2.1 Analyzing Emerging Threats and Attack Patterns 81
4.2.2 Creating Dynamic and Adaptive Training Content 83
4.2.3 Example 85
4.3 Enhancing Realism Through AI-Generated Elements 86
4.3.1 Creating Believable Digital Artifacts 87
4.3.2 Simulating Human Behavior in Threat Scenarios 90
4.4 Measuring and Improving Scenario Effectiveness 93
4.4.1 Analyzing Learner Performance and Engagement 93
4.4.2 Continuous Refinement of AI-Generated Scenarios 95
4.5 Ethical Considerations in AI-Generated Threat Scenarios 96
4.5.1 Ensuring Responsible Scenario Design 96
4.5.2 Balancing Realism with Learner Well-Being 97
References 99

5 AI-Enhanced Virtual and Augmented Reality for Cybersecurity Training 101
5.1 The Potential of VR and AR in Cybersecurity Training 101
5.1.1 Providing Realistic and Engaging Learning Environments 102
5.1.2 Enabling Hands-On Practice and Skill Development 104
5.2 AI-Driven Enhancements in VR and AR Training 105
5.2.1 Intelligent Interaction and Feedback Mechanisms 106
5.2.2 Adaptive Difficulty and Personalized Challenges 107
5.2.3 Automated Assessment and Performance Tracking 108
5.3 Designing Effective VR and AR Cybersecurity Training Modules 110
5.3.1 Identifying Key Learning Objectives and Scenarios 110
5.3.2 Balancing Realism and Usability 112
5.3.3 Integrating AI-Powered Features and Functionalities 114

5.4	Security Risks of VR and AR in Training Environments.........		116
	5.4.1	Vulnerabilities in VR and AR Hardware...............	116
	5.4.2	Data Privacy and Security Concerns..................	118
	5.4.3	Mitigating Risks in VR and AR Cybersecurity Training...	120
5.5	Future Trends and Innovations in VR/AR Cybersecurity Training...		121
	5.5.1	Integration with Other Emerging Technologies..........	121
	5.5.2	Advancements in AI-Driven VR/AR Training Scenarios..	124
	5.5.3	Overcoming Current Limitations and Challenges........	127
References...			129

Chapter 1
Introduction to AI in Cybersecurity Training

This chapter lays the foundation for understanding how artificial intelligence (AI) is poised to revolutionize the field of cybersecurity training. As digital threats become increasingly sophisticated and pervasive, the traditional methods of cybersecurity training struggle to keep pace. This chapter explores the transformative potential of AI in enhancing cybersecurity training practices, making them more adaptive, engaging, and effective. Through a detailed examination of the evolving landscape of cyber threats, the critical need for effective training, and the specific roles AI can play in this evolution, this chapter sets the stage for a deeper discussion on integrating AI into cybersecurity strategies.

This chapter provides a comprehensive overview of the transformative role of AI in revolutionizing cybersecurity training, addressing the evolving landscape of cyber threats that have progressed from simple viruses to complex, multi-vector attacks like ransomware, deepfakes, and AI-driven phishing. As digital technologies become more ingrained in everyday life and business operations, the need for effective cybersecurity training becomes more critical. This section highlights the dual necessity of building a resilient and vigilant workforce capable of acting as the first line of defense against cyber threats and reducing the risk and impact of cyber incidents through proactive and reactive training measures. It further explores how AI can dramatically enhance cybersecurity training by offering adaptive, personalized learning experiences, creating immersive and engaging training environments, and ensuring continuous improvement and relevance of training content to keep pace with rapidly evolving cyber threats and techniques.

The integration of AI into cybersecurity training is not merely an enhancement—it's a necessary evolution to address the complexity and dynamic nature of modern cyber threats. Providing adaptive, personalized learning experiences, creating engaging training environments, and ensuring the continuous relevance of content, AI can empower cybersecurity professionals and the organizations they protect. This chapter aims to illustrate the "why" and "how" AI should be integrated into cybersecurity training, setting the groundwork for more detailed discussions in

© The Author(s), under exclusive license to Springer Nature Switzerland AG 2025
S. Rana, R. Chicone, *Fortifying the Future*,
https://doi.org/10.1007/978-3-031-81780-9_1

subsequent chapters about specific AI technologies and their applications in cybersecurity.

1.1 The Evolving Landscape of Cyber Threats

The realm of cybersecurity has undergone significant transformations since the early days of simple computer viruses and network intrusions. As we navigate through 2024, the complexity and frequency of cyberattacks have escalated, profoundly impacting every sphere of modern society.[1] This evolution paints a vivid picture of how cyber threats have grown from mere annoyances to sophisticated strategies capable of crippling entire industries.

In the beginning, cyber threats were primarily basic viruses and worms, often created by hobbyists and pranksters. These were designed to exploit limited internet-connected systems. However, as technology advanced and digital connectivity became ubiquitous, so did the opportunities for malicious actors. Today, cyber threats encompass a wide array of sophisticated attacks such as ransomware, state-sponsored hacking, and IoT device breaches.

Ransomware has become one of the most prevalent and damaging types of cyber threats.[2] Initially, it involved encrypting an individual's or organization's data and demanding payment for the decryption key. Over time, this tactic has evolved into what is known today as double and triple extortion schemes. These do not merely stop at encryption; after initial encryption, attackers threaten to release the stolen data publicly if the ransom is not paid, adding an extra layer of extortion by threatening to inform customers or stakeholders about the breach, thereby leveraging reputation damage as another form of pressure.

These advanced ransomware tactics have led to significant disruptions in various sectors, with healthcare becoming an increasingly favored target. High-profile breaches like those at Change Healthcare[3] and Ascension[4] have showcased the vulnerability of healthcare institutions. These entities manage vast amounts of sensitive data and require high availability of their systems, making them prime targets for attackers seeking quick payouts or massive disruptions.

---

[1] Threat Landscape Report 2024. CyberArk. https://www.cyberark.com/resources/ebooks/identity-security-threat-landscape-2024-report

[2] Pearson, J. 2024, June 10th. Ransomware is 'More Brutal' Than Ever in 2024. Wired. https://www.wired.com/story/state-of-ransomware-2024/

[3] https://www.hhs.gov/hipaa/for-professionals/special-topics/change-healthcare-cybersecurity-incident-frequently-asked-questions/index.html

[4] https://about.ascension.org/en/cybersecurity-event

1.1 The Evolving Landscape of Cyber Threats

The incorporation of AI in cyber threats marks a pivotal development in the landscape. AI can help solve traffic jams and lessen emissions[5]—so why can't it help with cybersecurity?

AI-driven attacks can automate the process of finding vulnerabilities, crafting phishing emails that are incredibly convincing, or even impersonating trusted individuals in what are known as deepfake scams. Furthermore, AI-powered tools lower the barrier of entry for attackers, making attacks more ubiquitous. Moreover, the Internet of Things (IoT)[6] has expanded the attack surface dramatically. With billions of connected devices, from home thermostats to industrial control systems, each represents a potential entry point for malicious activities. Beyond financial motives, cybercrimes are increasingly driven by political, ideological, or even personal reasons. State-sponsored attacks seek to steal intellectual property, influence elections, or destabilize economies. Hacktivism also continues to rise, with groups breaking into systems to promote political agendas or social justice issues.

Addressing these multifaceted motivations requires an understanding of the psychology behind cyberattacks, a field still in its infancy. Moreover, researchers are also focusing on the psychological triggers and rewards for cybercriminals. Thus, allowing for security professionals to develop more effective countermeasures. However, our progress in this area is slow, and as our dependency on digital infrastructure grows, so does the rate at which it is targeted. Critical infrastructures like power grids, water systems, healthcare, educational institutions, transportation networks, and more face daily threats (and in some cases hourly threats) that could have catastrophic consequences. Moreover, the risks are not evenly distributed; vulnerable populations—whether due to economic, social, or political factors—are often less equipped to secure their systems and more susceptible to cyber extortion or fraud. This uneven vulnerability landscape underscores the pressing need for inclusive cybersecurity solutions that protect all segments of society.

All in all, AI has the potential to simulate a range of attack scenarios, adapt training modules in real-time, and provide cybersecurity professionals with the hands-on experience needed to combat these modern threats effectively. As we move forward, leveraging AI in cybersecurity education and defense will be crucial in staying a step ahead of malicious actors and safeguarding our digital and physical worlds against the sophisticated threats of the future.

---

[5] https://www.wsj.com/tech/personal-tech/google-green-light-traffic-light-optimization-992e4252?st=eixmtwxmuylup7x&reflink=desktopwebshare_permalink&utm_source=superhuman&utm_medium=newsletter&utm_campaign=how-ai-could-help-us-avoid-traffic-jams

[6] Lee, I. (2020). Internet of Things (IoT) cybersecurity: Literature review and IoT cyber risk management. *Future internet*, *12*(9), 157.

1.2 The Importance of Effective Cybersecurity Training

In today's digital era, marked by increasing technological advancements and sophisticated cyber threats, effective cybersecurity training stands as the primary defense against a myriad of security challenges.[7] This training is crucial not only for securing organizational assets but also for safeguarding individual privacy and maintaining public trust in digital systems. Moreover, as cyber threats evolve in complexity and subtlety, the role of effective cybersecurity training becomes more critical. Such training is the cornerstone of a secure digital landscape, equipping individuals with the knowledge and skills necessary to protect themselves and their organizations from cyber threats. Building a resilient and vigilant workforce can allow organizations to not only reduce the frequency and impact of cyber incidents but also strengthen the overall security posture of our interconnected world. This approach, when implemented effectively, prepares individuals to question discrepancies and recognize the subtleties of digital fraud, making cybersecurity a fundamental aspect of organizational culture and individual behavior.

1.2.1 Building a Resilient and Vigilant Workforce

The human factor is often cited as the weakest link in cybersecurity.[8] Despite advances in technology, human errors or lack of awareness can lead to significant security breaches. Traditional cybersecurity training methods have been criticized for being boring, monotonous[9] and ineffective,[10] often failing to bring about the necessary behavioral change among employees. Employees might still resort to jotting down passwords on sticky notes or using simplistic passwords like "password," (please don't do that anymore) indicating a grave lapse in adhering to security protocols. This is especially true in environments that does not have a mature security architecture. Small to medium sized entities (SMEs) often face this challenge if there are not adequate security controls and safeguards in place.

One illustrative example of the necessity for such training is the rise of deepfake technology, which has been used to impersonate executives in virtual meetings,

---

[7] Tolossa, Dawit. "Importance of cybersecurity awareness training for employees in business." *VIDYA-A JOURNAL OF GUJARAT UNIVERSITY* 2.2 (2023): 104–107.

[8] Goh, P. (2021). Humans as the weakest link in maintaining cybersecurity: Building cyber resilience in humans. In *Introduction to cyber forensic psychology: Understanding the mind of the cyber deviant perpetrators* (pp. 287–305).

[9] Cryer, J., & Zounlome, R. (2018). Cybersecurity: Bridging the gap between training and the effective knowledge base of employees in cyberthreat mitigation. *IU South Bend Undergraduate Research Journal, 18*, 7–17.

[10] Fagbule, O. (2023). *Cyber Security Training in Small to Medium-sized Enterprises (SMEs): Exploring Organisation Culture and Employee Training Needs* (Doctoral dissertation, Bournemouth University).

leading to frauds that have cost companies millions of dollars. In such cases, employees trained to detect anomalies in digital interactions could prevent potential disasters.

It is essential for cybersecurity training to explain the "why" behind security protocols, which often seem to complicate daily tasks. Understanding the rationale behind these measures can encourage adherence and foster a culture of security.[11] Integrating real-life scenarios and recent cyber incidents into training programs can make the risks more tangible and the need for strict security measures clearer.

Aligning with national strategies, such as the National Cybersecurity Strategy of 2023,[12] which aims to bolster resilience in critical infrastructure, is another crucial step. This alignment ensures that organizational practices are not only compliant with regulatory standards but also contribute to broader national security goals. Training programs must therefore evolve to teach employees how to remain vigilant in an environment where threats are not always perceptible and conventional senses might not be reliable indicators of authenticity.

1.2.2 Reducing the Risk and Impact of Cyber Incidents

Effective cybersecurity training significantly mitigates the risks associated with cyber threats. Educating individuals on the latest tactics used by cybercriminals, such as social engineering, malware attacks, and advanced phishing scams, allows them to be better prepared to recognize and respond to these threats proactively. This training also highlights the interdependent nature of modern digital ecosystems. In many cases, a breach in one part of a system can lead to widespread disruptions across different sectors due to the interconnectedness of digital infrastructures. Thus, comprehensive cybersecurity training is not only about protecting an individual's or an organization's data but also about safeguarding the entire digital and physical infrastructure they interact with.

Moreover, effective training personalizes the risks of cyber incidents, making it clear that everyone has a stake in cybersecurity.[13] It's not just organizations that suffer when a breach occurs; individuals can face significant personal and financial harm. Emphasizing personal responsibility and the collective benefits of cybersecurity allows training programs to foster a more conscientious approach to digital interactions.

---

[11] Uchendu, B., Nurse, J. R., Bada, M., & Furnell, S. (2021). Developing a cyber security culture: Current practices and future needs. *Computers & Security, 109*, 102,387.

[12] https://www.whitehouse.gov/wp-content/uploads/2023/03/National-Cybersecurity-Strategy-2023.pdf

[13] Beuran, Razvan, et al. "Towards effective cybersecurity education and training." (2016).

1.3 The Role of AI in Transforming Cybersecurity Training

Now that we've established the importance of cybersecurity training (and effective training at that) to address our evolving cyber landscape, it's important to understand the role that emerging technologies can play in assisting with the aforementioned. Specifically, how AI can assist in transforming cybersecurity training, which is not as effective as it could be in changing user behaviors and creating a more robust security perimeter.

The rapid advancement of technology has brought about significant changes in the digital landscape, and with it, an increased risk of cyber threats. As organizations strive to protect their assets and sensitive information, cybersecurity training has become a critical component of their defense strategy. However, traditional cybersecurity training methods often fall short in engaging employees and effectively preparing them to deal with the ever-evolving threat landscape. This is where AI comes into play, offering a transformative approach to cybersecurity training that can foster a culture of security and serve as a vital defense mechanism for users.

One of the most significant advantages of AI in cybersecurity training is its ability to provide personalized learning experiences.[14] Leveraging machine learning (ML) algorithms, AI-powered training systems can analyze individual learners' strengths, weaknesses, and learning styles, tailoring the content and pace to their specific needs. This personalized approach ensures that employees receive training that is relevant to their roles and addresses their knowledge gaps effectively. Thus, engaging learners with content that resonates with them, AI-driven training can significantly improve knowledge retention and practical application of cybersecurity best practices.

In the diverse landscape of learning, it's widely recognized that people absorb and process information differently. This diversity in learning styles—ranging from visual and auditory to kinesthetic—necessitates a flexible approach to education, particularly in complex fields like cybersecurity. Traditional one-size-fits-all training methods often fall short because they fail to address the unique learning preferences of each individual. This is where AI can make a profound impact, offering tailored educational experiences that enhance learning outcomes.

AI technologies have the capability to analyze the learning habits and performance of individuals, thereby identifying the most effective teaching methods for each learner. For instance, visual learners, who comprehend information better through images and spatial understanding, can benefit significantly from AI-generated infographics,[15] diagrams, and interactive simulations. These visual aids can make complex cybersecurity concepts more tangible and easier to

---

[14] Jawhar, Shadi, Jeremy Miller, and Zeina Bitar. "AI-Driven Customized Cyber Security Training and Awareness." *2024 IEEE 3rd International Conference on AI in Cybersecurity (ICAIC)*. IEEE, 2024.

[15] Nuhoğlu Kibar, Pınar. "Infographic creation as an essential skill for highly visual Gen Alpha." *Journal of Visual Literacy* (2024): 1–6.

understand. Similarly, AI can produce customized audio-visual presentations for auditory learners or interactive, scenario-based activities for kinesthetic learners who grasp knowledge best through hands-on experiences. Let's give an example here. Imagine we see someone who is not practicing physical security and keeps their computer unlocked while they are not at their desk. We can quickly go to our LLM of choice, let's say, DALL-E, and give it a prompt for an infographic.

Prompt:

"Create a simple infographic about locking your computer when you are away from your desk. Please make it like an oil painting with pastel colors so that it is pretty to look at and informative. Something I could print out."

Output:

It's that simple, the whole process took around 1 and a half minutes. Whereas before, one would have to go in and actually create an infographic that conveys what you would want. And remember, this will just continue to get better as time goes on.

Moreover, AI can dynamically adjust the complexity and format of content based on the learner's progress and feedback. This adaptive learning approach not only keeps the material engaging but also ensures that all learners, regardless of their cognitive preferences or abilities, can advance at their own pace and with optimal support. AI can cater to the diverse spectrum of learning styles; thus, allowing cybersecurity training to become more inclusive, effective, and empowering, equipping individuals with the skills and knowledge they need to navigate the increasingly complex digital world.

AI can create immersive and engaging training environments that captivate learners and make cybersecurity education more enjoyable. Through the use of gamification,[16] virtual reality, and interactive simulations, AI-powered training platforms can provide hands-on experiences that mimic real-world scenarios. These immersive environments allow employees to practice their skills in a safe and controlled setting, helping them develop the confidence and expertise needed to handle actual cyber threats. AI can transform cybersecurity education from a mundane chore to an exciting and rewarding experience, ultimately leading to better learning outcomes and a more security-conscious workforce. This can be done by making training more engaging and interactive—key variables that dictate the outcomes of learning.

Another crucial aspect of AI in cybersecurity training is its ability to ensure continuous improvement and relevance in the face of the ever-changing cyber threat landscape. Traditional training methods often rely on static content that quickly becomes outdated as new threats emerge and attack vectors evolve. AI, on the other hand, can continuously monitor the latest cybersecurity trends, threat intelligence, and real-world incidents, automatically updating training content to reflect the most current and relevant information. This dynamic approach ensures that employees receive up-to-date knowledge and skills, enabling them to effectively defend against the latest cyber threats.

Furthermore, AI can facilitate the creation of a strong cybersecurity culture within organizations. AI-powered training systems can help employees identify areas for improvement and encourage them to take proactive steps to enhance their cybersecurity knowledge and practices by providing personalized feedback and recommendations based on individual performance.[17] This continuous feedback loop fosters a sense of personal responsibility and accountability, empowering employees to become active participants in the organization's security posture. As a result, AI-driven training can cultivate a culture where cybersecurity is not just a mandate but a shared value that permeates all levels of the organization.

Thus, AI has the potential to revolutionize cybersecurity training, transforming it from a tedious and ineffective endeavor into a dynamic, engaging, and highly relevant experience. Leveraging personalized learning, immersive environments, and continuous improvement is important for AI-powered training to equip employees with the knowledge and skills necessary to defend against the ever-evolving cyber threat landscape. As organizations increasingly recognize the importance of a strong cybersecurity culture, AI will undoubtedly play a pivotal role in shaping the future of cybersecurity training, serving as a critical defense mechanism for users and organizations alike.

---

[16] Bezzina, Stephen, and Alexiei Dingli. "Rethinking gamification through artificial intelligence." *International Conference on Human-Computer Interaction.* Cham: Springer Nature Switzerland, 2023.

[17] Ansari, Meraj Farheen. "A quantitative study of risk scores and the effectiveness of AI-based Cybersecurity Awareness Training Programs." *International Journal of Smart Sensor and Adhoc Network* 3.3 (2022): 1.

1.3 The Role of AI in Transforming Cybersecurity Training

1.3.1 Adaptive and Personalized Learning Experiences

Adaptive and personalized learning experiences are a benefit of AI-powered cybersecurity training. It is important to understand the implications of the aforementioned and what it means exactly. As established, cybersecurity has become a critical concern for organizations across all industries. As cyber threats continue to grow in sophistication and frequency, it is essential to equip employees with the knowledge and skills necessary to protect sensitive data and maintain a robust security posture. However, traditional cybersecurity training methods often fall short in engaging learners and effectively preparing them to face real-world challenges. This is where adaptive and personalized learning experiences, powered by AI, can make a significant difference in cybersecurity training outcomes.

Adaptive learning is a key component in supporting positive learner outcomes, as it takes into account the individual needs and learning styles of each user.[18] Leveraging AI algorithms, adaptive learning systems can analyze a learner's performance, identify areas of strength and weakness, and dynamically adjust the content and pace of the training to optimize their learning experience. This approach ensures that learners receive the right level of challenge and support, allowing them to progress at their own pace and fully grasp the concepts being taught. Furthermore, this a more inclusive and accessible method of learning.

One of the most significant advantages of adaptive learning in cybersecurity training is its ability to cater to different learning preferences. Some individuals may prefer visual aids and interactive simulations, while others may learn better through reading or hands-on practice. AI-powered adaptive learning systems can recognize these preferences and deliver content in a format that resonates with each learner, enhancing their engagement and retention of information. Adaptive learning can help learners develop a deeper understanding of cybersecurity concepts and their practical applications by providing a tailored learning experience. This type of tailored learning experience may not be possible in traditional training formats.

Adaptive learning encourages learners to explore topics that pique their interest, allowing them to go down the "rabbit hole" and gain a more comprehensive understanding of cybersecurity. For example, if a learner shows a particular interest in social engineering tactics, the AI-powered system can present additional resources, case studies, and interactive scenarios related to that topic. This level of personalization not only keeps learners engaged but also helps them develop a well-rounded knowledge base that extends beyond the basic cybersecurity awareness training.

In addition to adaptive learning, personalized learning experiences are equally crucial in driving positive learner outcomes in cybersecurity training. Personalized learning goes beyond adapting the content and pace to individual needs; it also takes into account the learner's background, job role, and specific cybersecurity challenges they may face in their daily work. Personalized learning systems can create

---

[18] Gligorea, Ilie, et al. "Adaptive learning using artificial intelligence in e-learning: a literature review." *Education Sciences* 13.12 (2023): 1216.

unique learning paths for each user, ensuring that the training is highly relevant and applicable to their specific context. The aforementioned can be done by leveraging AI algorithms and machine learning,

AI-powered personalized learning experiences can simulate real-world scenarios and provide learners with opportunities to practice their skills in a safe and controlled environment.[19] For instance, an AI system can generate customized phishing emails or social engineering scenarios based on a learner's job role and the types of threats they are likely to encounter. Engaging in these interactive simulations allows learners to develop the practical skills and confidence needed to identify and respond to actual cyber threats in their work environment. Furthermore, AI-driven personalized learning can provide immediate feedback and guidance to learners, acting as a virtual tutor. As learners progress through the training, the AI system can offer real-time feedback on their performance, highlighting areas for improvement and providing targeted recommendations. This instant feedback loop allows learners to quickly identify and address any knowledge gaps, reinforcing their understanding of cybersecurity concepts and best practices.[20]

The flexibility offered by AI-powered adaptive and personalized learning is a key factor in driving positive learner outcomes. Traditional cybersecurity training often relies on static content delivered through webinars or classroom-style sessions, which can be inflexible and fail to engage learners effectively. In contrast, AI-driven learning systems can adapt to the learner's schedule, allowing them to access training materials at their convenience and progress at their own pace. This flexibility empowers learners to take ownership of their cybersecurity education and ensures that the training seamlessly integrates into their daily workflow.

Additionally, AI-powered cybersecurity training can continuously evolve and update its content based on the latest threat landscape and industry trends. As new cyber threats emerge and best practices change, the AI system can automatically incorporate this information into the training material, ensuring that learners always have access to the most current and relevant knowledge. This dynamic approach to cybersecurity training is essential in keeping pace with the ever-changing nature of cyber threats and equipping learners with the skills they need to defend against them.

1.3.1.1 Hypothetical Example: Emma & AI-Powered Cybersecurity Training for Personalized and Adaptive Cybersecurity Training

In order to conceptualize the aforementioned, let's go through a hypothetical example. Let's pretend there is a new employee, Emma, who is joining a financial institution. As part of her onboarding process, Emma is required to complete a cybersecurity training program powered by AI. When Emma begins the training, the

---

[19] Patkar, Mrs. Mrudula K. "Artificial intelligence and personalized learning." *Turkish Journal of Computer and Mathematics Education (TURCOMAT)* 12.13 (2021): 2411–2416.

[20] Ayeni, Oyebola Olusola, et al. "AI in education: A review of personalized learning and educational technology." *GSC Advanced Research and Reviews* 18.2 (2024): 261–271.

1.3 The Role of AI in Transforming Cybersecurity Training

AI system starts by assessing her existing knowledge and understanding of cybersecurity concepts through a series of interactive questions and scenarios. Based on her responses, the AI identifies that Emma has a strong grasp of basic security practices, such as creating strong passwords and identifying phishing emails, but struggles with more advanced topics like network security and data encryption.

Using this information, the AI-powered training system dynamically adapts the content and difficulty level to match Emma's needs. Instead of subjecting her to a generic, one-size-fits-all training program, the AI tailors the lessons to focus on the areas where Emma needs the most support. For example, the system might provide Emma with additional resources and explanations on network security concepts, while simply reinforcing her existing knowledge of password best practices.

As Emma progresses through the training, the AI system continues to monitor her performance and engagement. It notices that Emma tends to learn best through interactive simulations and hands-on practice. In response, the AI generates personalized scenarios that mimic the types of cybersecurity challenges Emma might face in her specific role at the financial institution. These simulations could include dealing with attempts to gain unauthorized access to sensitive financial data or responding to a suspected data breach.

Throughout the training, the AI provides Emma with immediate feedback and guidance. If she struggles with a particular concept or scenario, the AI offers targeted explanations and recommendations, acting as a virtual tutor. This real-time support helps Emma quickly overcome any obstacles and reinforces her learning.

Furthermore, the AI-powered system recognizes that Emma has a keen interest in social engineering tactics, as she spends more time exploring this topic and eagerly engages with related content. In response, the AI recommends additional resources and advanced training modules on social engineering, allowing Emma to dive deeper into this area and expand her knowledge beyond the standard curriculum. As Emma completes the training, the AI system provides her with a personalized summary of her strengths and areas for improvement. It also generates a customized action plan with recommendations for further learning and development based on her specific interests and job requirements.

Thanks to the adaptive and personalized learning experience provided by the AI-powered cybersecurity training, Emma not only gains a comprehensive understanding of critical cybersecurity concepts but also develops practical skills that are directly applicable to her role. She feels more confident in her ability to identify and respond to potential threats, and she is motivated to continue learning and staying up-to-date with the latest cybersecurity best practices.

In contrast to the AI-powered cybersecurity training that Emma experienced, traditional training methods often fail to deliver the same level of personalization and adaptability. With conventional training, Emma would likely be subjected to a standardized curriculum delivered through static presentations or pre-recorded videos. This one-size-fits-all approach fails to account for her individual learning needs, interests, and job-specific requirements. Without the real-time feedback, targeted recommendations, and interactive simulations offered by AI, Emma may struggle to fully grasp and retain the information presented. Traditional training lacks the ability to dynamically adjust content based on her performance and engagement, leading to a less effective learning experience. As a result, Emma may feel less motivated and ill-equipped to apply her newfound knowledge in real-world scenarios, ultimately compromising the organization's cybersecurity posture.

This hypothetical example demonstrates how AI-powered cybersecurity training can create a more engaging, effective, and personalized learning experience that caters to the unique needs and preferences of each individual learner, ultimately leading to better outcomes and a stronger cybersecurity posture for the organization as a whole. In general, adaptive and personalized learning experiences, powered by AI, have the potential to revolutionize cybersecurity training and drive positive learner outcomes. Catering to individual learning styles, providing tailored content, and offering interactive simulations and real-time feedback allows AI-driven learning systems to engage learners on a deeper level and help them develop a comprehensive understanding of cybersecurity concepts and best practices. As organizations increasingly recognize the importance of effective cybersecurity training, the adoption of AI-powered adaptive and personalized learning solutions will be crucial in building a strong cybersecurity culture and empowering employees to become the first line of defense against cyber threats.

1.3.2 Immersive and Engaging Training Environments

It is more critical than ever to ensure that individuals and organizations are well-prepared to face the challenges posed by cyber threats. Traditional cybersecurity training methods, such as meetings, webinars, lectures and static e-learning modules, often fall short in providing the necessary skills and knowledge to effectively defend against real-world attacks.[21] This is where AI-powered cybersecurity training comes into play, offering immersive and engaging training environments that can revolutionize the way we approach cybersecurity education.

1.3.2.1 The Importance of Immersive Environments in Cybersecurity Training

Immersive environments are crucial for effective cybersecurity training, as they allow learners to experience realistic scenarios and develop the skills needed to respond to stressful situations. In the context of cybersecurity, tabletop exercises and immersive simulations play a vital role in preparing individuals for the

---

[21] Angafor, Giddeon N., Iryna Yevseyeva, and Ying He. "Bridging the cyber security skills gap: Using tabletop exercises to solve the CSSG crisis." *Joint International Conference on Serious Games*. Cham: Springer International Publishing, 2020.

1.3 The Role of AI in Transforming Cybersecurity Training

challenges they may face in their daily work.[22] Cybersecurity professionals often find themselves in high-pressure situations where they must make quick decisions and take appropriate actions to mitigate risks and minimize damage. Immersive training environments provide a safe space for learners to practice these skills without the fear of real-world consequences. Thus, engaging in realistic simulations, learners can develop the muscle memory and mental resilience needed to respond effectively to cyber incidents.

Moreover, immersive training environments can help bridge the gap between theoretical knowledge and practical application. Cybersecurity concepts can be complex and abstract, making it difficult for learners to grasp their real-world implications. Through immersive experiences, learners can see firsthand how these concepts apply in practice, deepening their understanding and retention of the material. Many employers find that this is one of the major hurdles of hiring unskilled professionals—the fact that they do not have real world and hands on experience. Consequently, having immersive training environments can lend itself to more practical experiences and understanding of the issues found in the field and how to respond to them.[23]

The benefits of immersive environments extend beyond individual learning outcomes. It can create a workforce that is better prepared to handle cybersecurity challenges. Subsequently, organizations can strengthen their overall security posture. This is particularly important in light of the growing cybersecurity workforce gap, which has been identified as a significant national issue. The National Cybersecurity Strategy of 2023[24] and its implementation plan specifically address the need to develop a skilled and diverse cybersecurity workforce to meet the increasing demand for cybersecurity professionals.

1.3.2.2 AI-Powered Cybersecurity Training: Creating Immersive Experiences

AI-powered cybersecurity training is uniquely positioned to create immersive and engaging learning experiences. Leveraging advanced technologies such as virtual reality, augmented reality, and machine learning, AI-driven training platforms can generate realistic scenarios that closely mimic real-world cybersecurity challenges.[25] This will be discussed more in subsequent chapters of this book.

---

[22] Alnajim, Abdullah M., et al. "Exploring cybersecurity education and training techniques: a comprehensive review of traditional, virtual reality, and augmented reality approaches." *Symmetry* 15.12 (2023): 2175.

[23] Zhao, Jensen J., et al. "Enhancing organizational cybersecurity: A hands-on immersive learning project." *Issues Inf. Syst* 20.1 (2019): 100–107.

[24] https://www.whitehouse.gov/wp-content/uploads/2023/03/National-Cybersecurity-Strategy-2023.pdf

[25] Anwar, Muhammad Shahid, et al. "Immersive learning and AR/VR-based education: cybersecurity measures and risk management." *Cybersecurity Management in Education Technologies*. CRC

One of the key advantages of AI in creating immersive experiences is its ability to generate dynamic and adaptive content. Unlike traditional training methods that rely on pre-designed scenarios, AI-powered systems can create unique simulations tailored to each learner's needs and skill level. This adaptability ensures that learners are constantly challenged and engaged, promoting a deeper understanding of cybersecurity concepts. AI can also enhance the realism of immersive training environments by incorporating real-time threat intelligence and data from actual cyber incidents. The ability to analyze vast amounts of data on emerging threats and attack patterns, AI algorithms can generate simulations that reflect the latest trends and techniques used by cybercriminals. This ensures that learners are exposed to the most relevant and up-to-date scenarios, preparing them for the ever-evolving threat landscape.

Furthermore, AI-powered training platforms can provide immediate feedback and guidance to learners as they navigate through immersive simulations. The ability to analyze learners' actions and decisions allows AI algorithms can offer targeted recommendations and insights, helping individuals identify areas for improvement and refine their skills. This real-time feedback loop reinforces learning and allows learners to quickly adapt and improve their performance.

1.3.2.3 Engaging Training Environments: The Key to Changing User Behavior

Engagement is a critical factor in the success of cybersecurity training, as it directly impacts learners' motivation, retention, and application of knowledge.[26] AI-powered training solutions have the potential to revolutionize engagement levels in cybersecurity education, both for general cybersecurity awareness and specialized workforce training.[27]

One of the primary ways AI can enhance engagement is through personalization. AI-powered training platforms can analyze individual learners' preferences, learning styles, and performance data to create customized learning experiences, this can be done by leveraging ML. This personalization ensures that learners receive content and challenges that are relevant and engaging to them, increasing their motivation to actively participate in the training. AI can also introduce gamification elements into cybersecurity training, making the learning process more enjoyable and rewarding. Studies have demonstrated that gamification of cybersecurity training lends itself to more positive learner outcomes. Therefore, incorporating game-like features such as points, badges, and leaderboards, AI-powered platforms can tap into learners' natural desire for competition and achievement. This not only

---

Press, 2023. 1–22.

[26] Beuran, Razvan, et al. "Towards effective cybersecurity education and training." (2016).

[27] He, Wu, and Zuopeng Zhang. "Enterprise cybersecurity training and awareness programs: Recommendations for success." *Journal of Organizational Computing and Electronic Commerce* 29.4 (2019): 249–257.

1.3 The Role of AI in Transforming Cybersecurity Training

makes the training more engaging but also encourages learners to strive for better performance and continual improvement.

Moreover, AI-driven training solutions can create immersive storylines and narratives that contextualize cybersecurity concepts in relatable and meaningful ways. It can present information through compelling stories and real-world examples. Additionally, AI can help learners connect abstract concepts to practical applications, increasing their engagement and understanding. This storytelling approach is particularly effective in cybersecurity awareness training, where the goal is to change user behavior and foster a culture of security. Engaging training environments are crucial for driving behavioral change, as they encourage learners to actively interact with the material and internalize the lessons learned. When learners are engaged, they are more likely to retain information, apply it in their daily work, and adopt best practices for cybersecurity. This, in turn, leads to a more security-conscious workforce and a stronger overall security posture for the organization. It is also extremely beneficial in creating a culture of security, which is now one of the primary cybersecurity defenses we can have.

In summary, immersive and engaging training environments, powered by AI, are the key to effective cybersecurity training. Creating realistic simulations, providing personalized experiences, and leveraging gamification and storytelling elements allows AI-powered training solutions to revolutionize the way we approach cybersecurity education. These immersive and engaging environments not only improve individual learning outcomes but also contribute to closing the cybersecurity workforce gap and strengthening organizational security posture. As the threat landscape continues to evolve, embracing AI-powered cybersecurity training will be essential in developing a skilled and prepared workforce ready to face the challenges of the future.

1.3.2.4 Hypothetical Example: How AI-Powered Solutions Can Create Immersive & Engaging Environments

Let's say we have a large financial services company that has recently implemented an AI-powered cybersecurity training program. This is there to enhance employee's skills and preparedness. Now let's say we have a new cybersecurity analyze named Sarah. She begins her training journey by logging into the AI-powered training platform. The system greets Sarah and presents her with a personalized dashboard that outlines her training progress and recommends specific modules based on her job role and skill level.

As Sarah dives into the first module, she finds herself immersed in a realistic simulation of a cyber attack targeting the organization's network. The AI-generated scenario adapts in real-time to Sarah's actions, presenting her with challenges and decisions that closely mimic those she would face in a real-world incident. The training environment is visually rich and interactive, featuring virtual representations of the organization's systems, tools, and processes. Throughout the simulation, Sarah must apply her knowledge of cybersecurity concepts and best practices to detect, analyze, and mitigate the virtual attack. The AI provides context-sensitive guidance and feedback, helping Sarah understand the implications of her choices and offering suggestions for improvement. As she progresses, the AI adapts the difficulty level and introduces new challenges, ensuring that Sarah remains engaged and continues to develop her skills.

In addition to technical scenarios, the AI-powered training also includes modules focused on soft skills, such as communication and collaboration. Sarah participates in simulated team exercises where she must work with virtual colleagues to respond to a cyber incident. The AI generates realistic dialogue and team dynamics, allowing Sarah to practice effective communication and decision-making under pressure. Throughout the training, the AI tracks Sarah's performance and engagement, providing the organization's cybersecurity leaders with valuable insights into their team's strengths and areas for improvement. The platform also offers Sarah personalized recommendations for additional learning resources and real-world projects that align with her interests and career goals.

As Sarah completes the training modules, she feels more confident and prepared to handle real cybersecurity incidents. The immersive and engaging nature of the AI-powered training has allowed her to develop practical skills and experience in a safe, controlled environment. Sarah's enhanced capabilities, along with those of her colleagues who have undergone similar training, contribute to strengthening the organization's overall cybersecurity posture and resilience against evolving cyber threats. In contrast to the AI-powered cybersecurity training experience described above, traditional cybersecurity training often lacks the immersive and engaging qualities that are crucial for effective learning.

Current cybersecurity training often relies on passive, lecture-based approaches, such as classroom sessions or pre-recorded video courses. These methods typically present information in a linear, one-size-fits-all manner, failing to account for individual learners' needs, skill levels, and learning styles. Consequently, learners may find the content unengaging, leading to low retention rates and limited practical application of the knowledge gained. Moreover, traditional training rarely provides hands-on, interactive experiences that simulate real-world cybersecurity scenarios. Without the opportunity to practice and apply their skills in a realistic context, learners may struggle to translate theoretical knowledge into practical abilities, leaving them ill-prepared to handle actual cyber incidents. Unlike AI-powered training, which offers personalized feedback, adaptive challenges, and performance tracking, traditional methods often lack the means to assess and address individual learners' progress and areas for improvement. This absence of targeted support and guidance can hinder learners' growth and development. Consequently, traditional cybersecurity training often falls short in providing the immersive, engaging, and personalized experiences that are essential for effective skill development and knowledge retention.

1.3.3 Continuous Improvement and Relevance

In an era where cyber threats evolve with alarming speed and complexity, the traditional methods of cybersecurity training quickly become inadequate. The landscape demands not only current but continuously updated strategies to counteract emerging threats. This is where AI-powered solutions come into play, offering significant advantages over traditional training formats through the facilitation of continuous improvement in cybersecurity education.

Cybersecurity is a field defined by constant change. Continuous improvement in cybersecurity training is essential due to the dynamic nature of the threats themselves.[28] Cyber adversaries continually refine their methods and techniques, exploiting new vulnerabilities and adapting to security measures almost as quickly as they are implemented. In this high-stakes environment, cybersecurity training cannot remain static. It must evolve rapidly to keep pace with new threats, and this is particularly challenging with traditional training methods, which are often rigid and slow to update.

For individuals looking to enter the cybersecurity field, the fast-paced evolution of threats can be daunting. Continuous improvement through AI-driven training can help bridge the gap by providing up-to-date knowledge and skills relevant to the current threat landscape. Moreover, this approach can also address the workforce shortage in cybersecurity by enabling more efficient and effective training methods, thus preparing more professionals to enter the field quicker. One of the most pressing issues in cybersecurity is the workforce shortage. According to industry estimates, millions of cybersecurity positions remain unfilled worldwide, a gap that AI-powered solutions can help bridge. The barrier to entry for new learners can be significantly lowered. AI can adapt the complexity and depth of the content based on the learner's progress, making cybersecurity more accessible to a broader audience and helping to demystify the field for newcomers. It can lower the barrier of entry not just for attackers, but for those looking to enter the field as well!

AI-driven platforms can provide personalized learning paths that accommodate different learning styles and speeds, which is crucial for adult learners who may be transitioning from other careers. This personalized approach not only makes learning more efficient but also more engaging, which is vital for retaining learners in a field as demanding as cybersecurity.

What does continuous improvement look like? Continuous improvement in cybersecurity training involves regular updates to training modules, real-time adaptation to emerging threats, and the integration of recent case studies and technological advancements.[29] AI excels in these areas by leveraging data from current events and ongoing cybersecurity research to update and refine training materials

---

[28] Le, Hieu-Trung. *Meeting Cybersecurity Education Challenges: A Data Analytics Approach for Continuous Learning.* Diss. George Mason University, 2019.

[29] Hatzivasilis, George, et al. "Modern aspects of cyber-security training and continuous adaptation of programmes to trainees." *Applied Sciences* 10.16 (2020): 5702.

continuously. AI-powered solutions can analyze vast amounts of data to identify trends and predict which types of cyber threats are likely to become prominent. This predictive capability allows training programs to prepare learners for what they are most likely to encounter in the near future, rather than what was prevalent in the past. Moreover, AI can use feedback from training sessions to improve the content and delivery methods, ensuring that the training remains relevant and effective.

So, how does AI power continuous improvement? AI-powered solutions redefine the approach to cybersecurity training when it comes to adaptive learning, real-time content updates, scenario simulations, and feedback and analytics. AI can tailor training programs to the needs of individual learners, adjusting the complexity and pacing based on their performance and progress. This personalized learning approach not only makes training more effective but also ensures that all participants reach a competent level of knowledge and skill more efficiently. Unlike traditional training methods that require manual updates and revisions, AI systems can integrate the latest threat data and security trends as they emerge. This capability ensures that the training content remains relevant and that learners are always equipped with the latest knowledge to counteract new threats. Furthermore, AI can generate realistic cyber threat scenarios based on current events and emerging trends. These simulations provide practical, hands-on experience with the latest threats in a controlled environment, allowing learners to apply their knowledge and sharpen their problem-solving skills without real-world consequences. When it comes to feedback and analytics, AI systems can analyze the effectiveness of training modules by collecting data on learner engagement and performance. This feedback allows for the continuous refinement of training programs, ensuring they remain effective and engaging over time.

1.3.3.1 Enhancing Relevance and Efficiency with AI

One of the most significant advantages of AI-powered cybersecurity training is its ability to maintain relevance in a rapidly changing field. Traditional training methods often struggle to keep up due to the time, resources, and effort required to develop and update training materials. AI, however, can automate much of this process, significantly reducing the time and manpower needed to create and maintain training programs. For example, AI can quickly generate updated training scenarios that reflect the latest phishing techniques or ransomware threats, providing learners with the skills they need to address these issues as they arise in the real world. This timely relevance is crucial not only for training cybersecurity professionals but also for raising awareness among the general public. As more people become aware of how to recognize and respond to cyber threats, society as a whole becomes safer.

1.3.3.2 Impact on Learner Outcomes and the Cybersecurity Field

The implications of AI-powered solutions for cybersecurity training are profound. Thus, providing more relevant, personalized, and continuously updated training, AI can dramatically improve learner outcomes. Trainees are not only better prepared to handle current threats but also more adaptable to future challenges. This readiness is essential for building resilient cyber defenses and for developing a workforce capable of responding to an ever-changing threat landscape. Moreover, as AI-driven training becomes more widespread, it has the potential to revolutionize the field of cybersecurity. This is important in enabling more efficient training and better-prepared professionals. AI can help close the skills gap and strengthen the global response to cyber threats. This shift towards AI-powered training could be a key factor in safeguarding modern society against the cybersecurity challenges of tomorrow.

1.3.3.3 Hypothetical Scenario: Enhancing Continuous Improvement & Relevance with AI-Powered Cybersecurity Training

Let's go through another hypothetical scenario to help understand the conceptual into real world implementations. Consider the case of CyberSecure, a forward-thinking cybersecurity firm, where Mia, the head of the training department, recognizes the necessity for continuous improvement in their cybersecurity training programs. Given the dynamic nature of cyber threats, Mia decides to integrate AI-powered solutions to keep the company's training efforts both current and effective.

Mia's main goal is to ensure that CyberSecure's employees are not only well-prepared to handle existing threats but are also adaptive enough to tackle emerging challenges. To achieve this, she employs an AI-driven training platform that dynamically updates training modules based on the latest threat intelligence and cybersecurity trends. Mia starts by collaborating with an AI solutions provider to integrate a sophisticated AI system into CyberSecure's training infrastructure. The AI system is designed to scan thousands of data points from various cybersecurity feeds, incident reports, and threat databases to identify emerging threats.

Continuous Learning and Adaptation

Once integrated, the AI begins to function as both a curator and an instructor. It continuously analyzes new threats, such as the recent rise in ransomware attacks targeting remote access protocols, and quickly incorporates this data into the training curriculum. For instance, when a novel type of malware is detected proliferating in the financial sector, the AI system updates the training scenarios to include simulations and defensive strategies specific to this threat.

The AI also monitors the performance of trainees in real-time, adjusting the difficulty of simulations and quizzes based on individual and group performance metrics. If the AI detects that a particular group is struggling with concepts related to network security, it can automatically introduce additional modules or more comprehensive reviews on that topic.

Enhancing Relevance Through Real-Time Scenarios

One of Mia's innovative uses of AI is in creating real-time cyberattack simulations that mimic current events. For example, when a significant breach involving a zero-day exploit occurs, the AI quickly designs a training module that not only explains the exploit but also simulates an attack scenario based on the breach. This allows employees to practice their response strategies in a controlled, yet urgent and relevant environment. Mia ensures that the AI system is designed with a robust feedback loop. After each training session, employees provide feedback on the module's relevance and difficulty, which the AI uses to enhance future training content. This feedback loop also allows Mia to monitor the effectiveness of the training, making strategic adjustments to the AI's learning algorithms to better serve the company's needs.

So, what's the outcome?

Within several months of implementing the AI-powered training solution, CyberSecure notices a measurable improvement in their team's ability to respond to and mitigate cyber incidents. The training's relevance and adaptability keep the employees engaged and constantly learning, significantly boosting their confidence and competence in handling real-world cybersecurity challenges. If you think about it, this can set a new standard for how cybersecurity training can be dynamically adapted in response to an ever-changing threat landscape.

1.3.4 Generative AI in Cybersecurity Training

Differentiating between generative AI and other forms of AI in the context of cybersecurity training is crucial due to the distinct roles and capabilities each type of technology offers. This differentiation helps in selecting the right AI tools for specific training needs, optimizing the effectiveness of training programs, and addressing unique cybersecurity challenges.[30] Generative AI specializes in creating content and scenarios dynamically based on input data, which makes it particularly useful for developing realistic cybersecurity simulations and training modules. This contrasts with other forms of AI, such as analytical AI, which might focus more on

---

[30] Nowrozy, Raza, and David Jam. "Embracing the generative AI revolution: Advancing tertiary education in cybersecurity with GPT." *arXiv preprint arXiv:2403.11402* (2024).

processing large datasets to identify trends or anomalies in network traffic. Understanding these distinctions ensures that the AI technology deployed is best suited to the training objectives, whether that's generating engaging educational content or analyzing security vulnerabilities.

Generative AI can automatically generate training scenarios that are highly realistic and continuously evolving, closely mirroring the fast-changing landscape of cyber threats. This capability is vital for preparing trainees for the kinds of complex and adaptive challenges they will face in the real world. In contrast, other forms of AI might be used to reinforce learning through repetition or to optimize the learning path based on performance metrics. Knowing when to use generative AI for scenario generation versus when to use other AI forms for learning optimization or performance tracking can significantly enhance the training's relevance and effectiveness. Generative AI has a unique capacity to create engaging, interactive, and rich multimedia content. This can significantly boost learner engagement and improve retention rates by providing a more immersive learning experience. This is different from other AI applications that might focus on assessing learner performance or providing feedback, which, while also crucial, do not directly contribute to the immersive quality of the training content.

The use of generative AI in cybersecurity training allows for a high degree of personalization and adaptability in training programs. It can analyze individual performance and tailor the difficulty and type of content to meet each learner's specific needs. This level of customization is vital in ensuring that all learners, regardless of their initial skill level, can benefit from the training. Other AI technologies might be deployed in more static roles, such as monitoring completion rates or scoring assessments, which are less dynamic but still essential to the overall training framework. Generative AI can streamline the creation of training materials and simulations, making it easier and more cost-effective to scale up cybersecurity training initiatives to accommodate more learners or to diversify training offerings. This is especially important in large organizations or in environments where cyber threats evolve rapidly. Other forms of AI might help scale in different ways, such as by automating the evaluation process or facilitating large-scale data analysis, which also contributes to the overall efficiency but in a different context.

Understanding the specific contributions of generative AI versus other types of AI allows organizations to strategically deploy these technologies to maximize their impact in cybersecurity training. It helps in making informed decisions about technology investments and in designing training programs that are not only comprehensive and effective but also efficient and tailored to the needs of the learners. The ability to distinguish between these different AI applications ensures that cybersecurity training is not just a routine educational requirement but a strategic, adaptive, and continuously improving initiative.

Thus, Generative AI is transforming the landscape of cybersecurity training and awareness by providing dynamic, tailored, and highly engaging educational experiences. This technology not only adapts to the needs and progress of learners but also ensures that the content remains at the cutting edge of the cybersecurity field. One of the standout features of generative AI in cybersecurity training is its ability to create realistic, adaptive cyber threat scenarios. This capability allows learners to experience near-real-world challenges within a controlled environment, enhancing their ability to respond to actual threats. Generative AI algorithms can simulate a broad spectrum of cyber threats, from basic phishing attacks to complex, multi-layered ransomware attacks, based on real-time data and emerging trends. This prepares learners not just for the threats of today but also for future challenges, making training proactive rather than reactive. The adaptiveness of these simulations means that they can change in response to the learner's actions, providing a truly interactive experience that tests decision-making skills under pressure. For example, if a learner successfully thwarts an initial hacking attempt, the AI might escalate the scenario to include secondary fallback attacks, mimicking the persistence and evolving tactics of real-world attackers.

Generative AI excels in creating personalized learning experiences by analyzing each learner's performance continuously. It identifies individual knowledge gaps and skill deficiencies, allowing the training program to target specific areas where a learner may need more focus or additional practice. This is achieved through sophisticated algorithms that assess responses, track progress, and adjust the difficulty of tasks accordingly. For instance, if a learner struggles with network security concepts, the AI can provide additional resources, such as targeted readings, interactive simulations, and custom quizzes, to aid in comprehension. This level of personalization ensures that all learners, regardless of their starting knowledge or skill level, receive the education they need to advance their proficiency in cybersecurity.

Generative AI also significantly enhances the quality of educational content by producing interactive, multimedia-rich training materials. These can include video tutorials that adapt the pacing based on learner engagement, interactive infographics that delve deeper into complex data as the user interacts with them, and gamified elements that make learning more enjoyable and memorable. This type of content not only makes the learning process more engaging but also helps in the retention of knowledge and the development of practical skills. For example, an AI-generated module might include a virtual lab where learners can practice configuring security protocols on a simulated network, receiving instant feedback and tips generated by AI. This hands-on approach ensures that learners not only understand theoretical concepts but can also apply them in practical settings.

Lastly, generative AI keeps cybersecurity training relevant by continuously incorporating the latest threat intelligence into the curriculum. As new vulnerabilities are discovered and new forms of cyberattacks are developed, AI systems can instantly update training modules to include information and defense strategies against these emerging threats. This ensures that learners are always up-to-date with the current landscape of cybersecurity challenges. For example, if a new type of malware starts spreading globally, the AI system can quickly generate training modules that explain the malware's mechanics, show how it spreads, and simulate scenarios where learners must stop an infection. This not only prepares learners to handle current threats but also instills a culture of continuous learning and adaptation, which is crucial in the fast-evolving domain of cybersecurity.

1.4 Conclusion of This Chapter

As we conclude this chapter, it is clear that the integration of AI into cybersecurity training is not merely a futuristic ideal but a necessary evolution to effectively combat the sophisticated and rapidly evolving cyber threats of today. The diverse capabilities of AI, from personalizing learning experiences to simulating complex cyber scenarios, underscore its critical role in preparing a workforce that is both vigilant and adaptive. The continuous update of training content ensures that cybersecurity professionals are not only equipped to handle current threats but are also prepared for emerging challenges, thereby safeguarding digital assets and sensitive information across various sectors.

Furthermore, the transformation brought about by AI in cybersecurity training aligns perfectly with the need for a strategic approach that accommodates the dynamic nature of cyber threats. AI ensures that learning is both effective and enduring, making cybersecurity awareness and defense second nature to individuals within an organization. This foundational understanding sets the stage for deeper exploration in the subsequent chapters, particularly focusing on how AI can power adaptive learning systems that are finely tuned to the needs, skill levels, and progress of each learner.

Looking ahead to the next chapter, we will delve into the specifics of AI-powered adaptive learning systems in cybersecurity training. The next chapter aims to illuminate how these systems not only adjust content based on real-time assessments of learner performance but also how they can forecast potential learning gaps and preemptively tailor the training process. This proactive approach not only maximizes learning efficiency but also significantly enhances the strategic preparedness of organizations against cyber threats, marking a pivotal shift in how cybersecurity training is conceptualized and delivered.

References

1. Threat Landscape Report. (2024). *CyberArk*. https://www.cyberark.com/resources/ebooks/identity-security-threat-landscape-2024-report
2. Pearson, J. (2024, June 10). *Ransomware is 'More Brutal' than ever in 2024*. Wired. https://www.wired.com/story/state-of-ransomware-2024/
3. https://www.hhs.gov/hipaa/for-professionals/special-topics/change-healthcare-cybersecurity-incident-frequently-asked-questions/index.html
4. https://about.ascension.org/en/cybersecurity-event
5. https://www.wsj.com/tech/personal-tech/google-green-light-traffic-light-optimization-992e4252?st=eixmtwxmuylup7x&reflink=desktopwebshare_permalink&utm_source=superhuman&utm_medium=newsletter&utm_campaign=how-ai-could-help-us-avoid-traffic-jams
6. Lee, I. (2020). Internet of Things (IoT) cybersecurity: Literature review and IoT cyber risk management. *Future Internet, 12*(9), 157.
7. Tolossa, D. (2023). Importance of cybersecurity awareness training for employees in business. *Vidya-A Journal of Gujarat University, 2*(2), 104–107.

8. Goh, P. (2021). Humans as the weakest link in maintaining cybersecurity: Building cyber resilience in humans. In *Introduction to cyber forensic psychology: Understanding the mind of the cyber deviant perpetrators* (pp. 287–305).
9. Cryer, J., & Zounlome, R. (2018). Cybersecurity: Bridging the gap between training and the effective knowledge base of employees in cyberthreat mitigation. *IU South Bend Undergraduate Research Journal, 18*, 7–17.
10. Fagbule, O. (2023). *Cyber security training in small to medium-sized enterprises (SMEs): Exploring organisation culture and employee training needs* (Doctoral dissertation, Bournemouth University).
11. Uchendu, B., Nurse, J. R., Bada, M., & Furnell, S. (2021). Developing a cyber security culture: Current practices and future needs. *Computers & Security, 109*, 102387.
12. https://www.whitehouse.gov/wp-content/uploads/2023/03/National-Cybersecurity-Strategy-2023.pdf
13. Beuran, R, et al. (2016). *Towards effective cybersecurity education and training*
14. Jawhar, S., Miller, J., & Bitar, Z. (2024). AI-driven customized cyber security training and awareness. In *2024 IEEE 3rd international conference on AI in cybersecurity (ICAIC)*. IEEE.
15. Pınar, N. K. (2024). Infographic creation as an essential skill for highly visual gen alpha. *Journal of Visual Literacy*, 1–6.
16. Bezzina, S., & Dingli, A. (2023). Rethinking gamification through artificial intelligence. In *International conference on human-computer interaction*. Springer.
17. Ansari, M. F. (2022). A quantitative study of risk scores and the effectiveness of AI-based cybersecurity awareness training programs. *International Journal of Smart Sensor and Adhoc Network, 3*(3), 1.
18. Gligorea, I., et al. (2023). Adaptive learning using artificial intelligence in e-learning: A literature review. *Education Sciences, 13*(12), 1216.
19. Patkar, M. M. K. (2021). Artificial intelligence and personalized learning. *Turkish Journal of Computer and Mathematics Education (TURCOMAT), 12*(13), 2411–2416.
20. Ayeni, O. O., et al. (2024). AI in education: A review of personalized learning and educational technology. *GSC Advanced Research and Reviews, 18*(2), 261–271.
21. Angafor, G. N., Yevseyeva, I., & He, Y. (2020). Bridging the cyber security skills gap: Using tabletop exercises to solve the CSSG crisis. In *Joint international conference on serious games*. Springer.
22. Alnajim, Abdullah M., et al. *Exploring cybersecurity education and training techniques: A comprehensive review of traditional, virtual reality, and augmented reality.*
23. Zhao, J. J., et al. (2019). Enhancing organizational cybersecurity: A hands-on immersive learning project. *Issues Information Systems, 20*(1), 100–107.
24. National Cybersecurity Strategy. *White House.* https://www.whitehouse.gov/wp-content/uploads/2023/03/National-Cybersecurity-Strategy-2023.pdf
25. Anwar, M. S., et al. (2023). Immersive learning and AR/VR-based education: Cybersecurity measures and risk management. In *Cybersecurity Management in Education Technologies* (pp. 1–22). CRC Press.
26. He, W., & Zhang, Z. (2019). Enterprise cybersecurity training and awareness programs: Recommendations for success. *Journal of Organizational Computing and Electronic Commerce, 29*(4), 249–257.
27. Le, H.-T. (2019). *Meeting cybersecurity education challenges: A data analytics approach for continuous learning.* Diss. George Mason University.
28. Hatzivasilis, G., et al. (2020). Modern aspects of cyber-security training and continuous adaptation of programmes to trainees. *Applied Sciences, 10*(16), 5702.
29. Nowrozy, R., & Jam, D. (2024). Embracing the generative AI revolution: Advancing tertiary education in cybersecurity with GPT. *arXiv preprint arXiv, 2403*, 11402.

Chapter 2
AI-Driven Personalized Learning in Cybersecurity Training

This chapter explores how AI can power adaptive learning systems that tailor training content to individual learner needs, skill levels, and progress.

The traditional one-size-fits-all approach to training is becoming increasingly ineffective. Cybersecurity, with its complex and ever-changing nature, requires a more tailored educational approach that can adapt to the unique needs, skills, and progress of each learner. This chapter delves into how AI-driven personalized learning systems are revolutionizing cybersecurity training by offering customized learning experiences that address individual knowledge gaps, enhance engagement and retention, and optimize learning outcomes.

One of the most significant advantages of personalized learning in cybersecurity training is its ability to identify and address individual knowledge gaps and skill deficiencies. Unlike traditional training methods that deliver the same content to every learner, AI-driven systems can assess each individual's current knowledge state and tailor the training content accordingly. This targeted approach ensures that learners are not wasting time on material they already know or missing out on crucial information they lack.

For instance, a new employee with a background in IT may have a strong grasp of basic network security but little understanding of recent developments in cryptographic security measures. An AI-driven system can identify this gap and adjust the training curriculum to focus on these areas, thereby making the learning experience much more efficient and effective. This personalized approach not only speeds up the learning process but also ensures a deeper understanding and proficiency in handling real-world cybersecurity challenges.

The detailed exploration of AI-driven personalized learning in cybersecurity training in this chapter underscores its importance and relevance in today's digital landscape. AI not only enhances the efficiency and effectiveness of cybersecurity training but also prepares a more competent and skilled workforce capable of addressing and mitigating the risks associated with current and future cyber threats. This chapter aims to lay a solid foundation for understanding how adaptive learning

© The Author(s), under exclusive license to Springer Nature Switzerland AG 2025
S. Rana, R. Chicone, *Fortifying the Future*,
https://doi.org/10.1007/978-3-031-81780-9_2

powered by AI can transform cybersecurity education and training, making it a critical tool in the development of robust cyber defenses for any organization.

2.1 The Benefits of Personalized Learning in Cybersecurity Training

In the domain of cybersecurity, where the threat landscape evolves at a pace that seems like it changes minute by minute, the traditional, one-size-fits-all approach to training is rapidly proving inadequate. This section delves into the critical advantages of personalized learning in cybersecurity training, highlighting how AI-driven approaches can address specific knowledge gaps and skill deficiencies, while simultaneously enhancing learner engagement and retention. This adaptive and tailored learning is essential not only for keeping pace with sophisticated cyber threats but also for equipping professionals with the necessary skills to defend against them effectively.

One of the foremost benefits of personalized learning, particularly in a field as specialized and dynamic as cybersecurity, is its ability to pinpoint and address individual knowledge gaps and skill deficiencies. Traditional training methods often fail to meet the unique needs of each learner, glossing over areas where some may need intensive support while unnecessarily reiterating topics that others have already mastered. In contrast, AI-driven personalized learning systems assess the specific capabilities and knowledge base of each learner, tailoring the content to fill gaps effectively.[1]

For instance, a professional might be proficient in detecting and mitigating malware but less knowledgeable about defending against social engineering attacks or the risks associated with scanning QR codes—a growing concern in today's digital environment. An AI system can identify these gaps through initial assessments and ongoing performance metrics, dynamically adjusting the training curriculum to address these deficiencies. This targeted approach ensures that all learners, regardless of their starting point, achieve a balanced and comprehensive understanding of current cyber threats.

AI-driven personalized learning transforms the educational experience by making it highly engaging and significantly more effective at retaining learners.[2] AI systems leverage data analytics to adapt the difficulty level and format of the content according to the learner's engagement levels, ensuring that the material is neither too challenging nor too simplistic. This customization keeps learners in a state

---

[1] Pratama, Muh Putra, Rigel Sampelolo, and Hans Lura. "Revolutionizing education: harnessing the power of artificial intelligence for personalized learning." *Klasikal: Journal of education, language teaching and science* 5.2 (2023): 350–357.

[2] Chang, Junming, and Xu Lu. "The study on students' participation in personalized learning under the background of artificial intelligence." *2019 10th International Conference on Information Technology in Medicine and Education (ITME)*. IEEE, 2019.

of optimal challenge, known as the flow state,³ which has been shown to enhance learning efficiency and retention.

Moreover, personalized learning through AI includes the use of interactive elements, such as simulations and gamified scenarios, which provide hands-on experience with real-world challenges. These elements are not only tailored to the learning needs and progress of each individual but are also updated continuously to reflect the latest cyber threats and tactics. This real-time updating not only maintains the relevance of the training material but also keeps learners engaged with the most current and pertinent issues facing the cybersecurity field today.

The integration of AI into personalized learning is not just an enhancement—it's a revolution in cybersecurity training. As cyber attackers continually advance their methods and knowledge, the defensive side must not only keep pace but also anticipate future threats. AI offers the potential to bridge this growing knowledge gap through its ability to learn and adapt quickly. Thus, with AI, cybersecurity training can evolve at a pace commensurate with that of cyber threats, thereby significantly narrowing the window of opportunity for attackers. This section emphasizes the importance of personalized learning as a critical component of modern cybersecurity training strategies. It addresses how AI can be specifically leveraged to pinpoint and close knowledge gaps across a diverse workforce and enhance engagement and retention through customized, relevant, and interactive training experiences. As we move forward, the ability to effectively utilize AI in training will be pivotal in developing a cybersecurity workforce capable of defending against an increasingly sophisticated array of cyber threats. Fully embracing AI-driven personalized learning allows the cybersecurity industry to not only keep pace with attackers but also gain a strategic advantage in the ongoing battle to secure digital assets and information.

2.1.1 Addressing Individual Knowledge Gaps and Skill Deficiencies

Based on the aforementioned, let's discuss how specifically AI can enhance cybersecurity training in terms of addressing individual knowledge gaps and skill deficiencies. Personalized learning has emerged as a critical solution for addressing the diverse and specific needs of learners. Traditional training methods often struggle to meet these needs due to their generalized approach, which can leave significant gaps in individual knowledge and skills.⁴ AI, however, offers a significant advancement

---

[3] Pavlas, Davin, et al. "Game-based learning: The impact of flow state and videogame self-efficacy." *Proceedings of the human factors and ergonomics society annual meeting*. Vol. 54. No. 28. Sage CA: Los Angeles, CA: SAGE Publications, 2010.
[4] Alnajim, Abdullah M., et al. "Exploring cybersecurity education and training techniques: a comprehensive review of traditional, virtual reality, and augmented reality approaches." *Symmetry* 15.12 (2023): 2175.

in training methodologies by providing personalized learning experiences tailored to the unique strengths and weaknesses of each individual. This section delves deeply into how AI can specifically address knowledge gaps and skill deficiencies, enhancing the overall competence and preparedness of the cybersecurity workforce.

2.1.1.1 The Limitations of Traditional Training Methods

Traditional cybersecurity training often involves static learning materials such as textbooks and one-size-fits-all lectures. These methods assume a uniformity in background knowledge and learning pace among students, which is rarely the case. In a group of even five learners, differences in understanding, skills, and experience levels can vary widely. Traditional trainers, no matter how skilled, cannot fully customize their approach to meet each learner's specific needs, and they themselves may not have expertise in all areas of cybersecurity, leading to gaps in the training content. Furthermore, traditional methods do not always accommodate different learning styles or provide the flexibility necessary for learners to progress at their own pace. This can result in learners either falling behind due to unaddressed knowledge gaps or becoming disengaged because the content is not challenging enough.

2.1.1.2 How AI Transforms Cybersecurity Training

AI-powered learning systems represent a paradigm shift in how training is designed and delivered. These systems can assess individual learning styles, knowledge levels, and performance data to create a highly personalized learning path for each user. AI systems can continuously assess a learner's performance and knowledge retention in real-time. Using algorithms to analyze test results, quiz responses, and interactive simulation performances, AI can identify specific areas where a learner is struggling and adjust the curriculum accordingly.

AI can create highly customized learning materials—who wishes they had this back in grade school? Based on the assessment, AI can generate personalized learning materials that focus on areas of deficiency. For learners who need more help with certain topics, such as network security protocols or recent phishing tactics, the AI can provide additional resources, such as targeted readings, interactive simulations, or explanatory videos. Multimodal learning is another benefit here. Recognizing that different people learn best through different means, AI can deliver content in various formats. For visual learners, it can create infographics and diagrams; for auditory learners, podcasts and audio explanations; and for kinesthetic learners, interactive labs and virtual reality environments. This flexibility not only makes learning more effective but also more engaging.

Now it's time for our hypothetical examples to help bridge the gap between the conceptual and what is able to be implemented.

2.1.1.3 Enhancing Knowledge with AI—The Case of Mia

Mia, a recent hire at a tech company (good job, Mia!), steps into her role with a robust background in software development. While her coding skills are top-notch, her experience with network security is considerably less developed—a gap that could hinder her effectiveness as a cybersecurity analyst. Recognizing this, her employer utilizes an AI-driven learning platform to craft a personalized training path that targets her specific needs.

The process begins with an initial diagnostic assessment, where Mia is tested on various aspects of cybersecurity to gauge her existing knowledge and identify areas lacking in depth. The AI system analyzes her responses using sophisticated algorithms that not only pinpoint deficiencies but also measure her learning style and pace. This initial data collection is critical as it sets the baseline from which her personalized learning journey is developed.

Once Mia's learning needs are clearly mapped out, the AI system curates a series of detailed educational modules focused specifically on network security. These modules cover a range of topics, from the basics of network architecture to advanced network threats and how to mitigate them. Each topic is broken down into digestible segments that Mia can work through at her own pace. To reinforce learning, the AI integrates various multimedia elements tailored to her preferred learning style, including video tutorials, interactive diagrams, and written guides.

Interactive simulations play a pivotal role in Mia's training. These simulations provide a safe, controlled environment where Mia can apply her newfound knowledge in practical scenarios. For instance, one simulation might task her with setting up and configuring firewalls to protect a network, while another challenges her to detect and respond to a simulated network intrusion. As Mia interacts with these simulations, the AI closely monitors her actions, providing real-time feedback and dynamically adjusting the complexity of the scenarios based on her performance.

This feedback is crucial for Mia's development. It not only points out areas where she needs further improvement but also highlights her strengths, helping build her confidence. As she progresses, the AI system continues to evolve her learning path, introducing more complex topics and simulations to ensure her continuous growth and readiness to handle real-world cybersecurity challenges effectively.

2.1.1.4 Addressing Skill Deficiencies: A Hypothetical Scenario—The Case of Jake

Jake, an IT professional with a decade of experience in system administration, is keen to pivot into a cybersecurity role. However, his direct experience with the advanced cybersecurity tools necessary for such a position is minimal. To facilitate his transition, his employer leverages an AI-driven training platform designed to bridge the gap between his current skill set and the demands of a cybersecurity job.

Jake's journey begins with an assessment similar to Mia's, designed to evaluate his understanding of basic cybersecurity concepts and his proficiency with various IT tools. This assessment helps the AI determine the starting point of his personalized learning path and ensures the training content is neither too basic nor overly advanced.

As Jake engages with his customized training program, he encounters a series of modules that introduce him to advanced cybersecurity tools and techniques. These modules are interactive and incorporate elements of gamification to maintain engagement. For example, Jake might use a virtual environment to learn how to use intrusion detection systems, participate in identifying vulnerabilities in software, or engage in exercises that teach him about forensic analysis following a cyber-attack.

Progressively challenging simulations are central to Jake's training. These simulations are designed to mimic real-world scenarios that Jake would face as a cybersecurity professional. Each task he completes is designed to build on the last, gradually increasing in complexity. As he progresses, the AI system continuously assesses his performance, adjusting the difficulty of the tasks to ensure they remain challenging but achievable.

The AI system not only keeps Jake engaged through these tailored tasks and simulations but also provides him with ongoing feedback. This feedback is detailed, highlighting areas where Jake excels and pinpointing where he needs more practice. Through this iterative process, Jake develops hands-on experience with the tools and scenarios he will encounter in his desired role, effectively bridging his skill deficiencies.

These examples of Mia and Jake illustrate the profound impact that AI-driven personalized learning can have on addressing individual knowledge gaps and skill deficiencies in cybersecurity training. Tailoring the learning experience to the specific needs of each individual, AI not only enhances knowledge and skills but also prepares learners for the specific challenges they will face in their roles. Thus, this significantly contributes to the broader goal of fortifying organizational cybersecurity.

2.1.2 Enhancing Learner Engagement and Retention

The challenge of engaging learners effectively and ensuring that the information is retained and applied has become increasingly prominent.[5] Traditional methods often fail to maintain learner engagement, which is critical for successful outcomes in training environments. AI in cybersecurity training has revolutionized this aspect by transforming how content is delivered, how learners interact with the material, and how training adapts to meet individual learner needs.

---

[5] Al-Daeef, Melad. "CHALLENGES OF THE SUCCESS OF CYBERSECURITY TRAINING PROGRAMS." *Journal of Basic Sciences* 35.2 (2022): 27–36.

2.1.2.1 The Importance of Engagement and Retention

Engagement[6] in learning, particularly in the field of cybersecurity, is more than just paying attention—it's about interacting meaningfully with the content. When learners are truly engaged, they are actively thinking about, interacting with, and applying what they are learning. This active involvement is crucial because it significantly enhances retention; the more a learner interacts with material, the more likely it is to stick. Retention is critical in cybersecurity training where the information learned must not only be recalled but also applied in real-world scenarios to protect against threats.

Moreover, engagement and retention are essential metrics for the success of any training program. They are the main variables that translate knowledge into behavior, crucial in an environment as dynamic and critical as cybersecurity. Without high levels of both, the risk of security lapses due to insufficient training increases dramatically.

As aforementioned, AI can analyze a learner's previous knowledge, pace of learning, and preferred learning styles to create customized learning paths. This personalization addresses the unique needs of each learner, which prevents the boredom and disengagement that can come from a one-size-fits-all approach. Presenting challenges that are neither too easy nor too difficult, AI keeps learners in an optimal state of engagement known as the "flow" state. AI-powered platforms can incorporate simulations, interactive content, and gamified elements into the training regimen. These interactive modules are not just more engaging than passive forms of learning; they also improve retention by allowing learners to practice what they learn in simulated real-world scenarios. For example, using VR to simulate a cyberattack scenario allows learners to experience the intensity and pressure of a live cybersecurity breach without the real-world risks. We will talk about that later in this book. AI systems provide immediate feedback—a critical component of effective learning. If a learner makes a mistake, AI can instantly offer corrections and explain the error, reinforcing learning through correction. Additionally, AI can adapt the difficulty level of the training based on the learner's performance, ensuring that they are always challenged but not overwhelmed.

Senior leaders, trainers, and trainees must understand the importance of AI in enhancing engagement and retention for several reasons. They need to allocate budget and resources effectively. Understanding that AI-driven training could lead to more efficient and effective cybersecurity practices helps justify the investment in advanced AI technologies for training purposes. Cybersecurity trainers also need to have awareness here. With AI's capabilities, trainers can focus on more strategic aspects of cybersecurity education, such as developing advanced cybersecurity scenarios or integrating the latest threats into simulations. This shift can make their work more impactful and satisfying. And of course, we cannot forget the trainees.

---

[6] Prümmer, Julia. "The Role of Cognition in Developing Successful Cybersecurity Training Programs–Passive vs. Active Engagement." *International Conference on Human-Computer Interaction*. Cham: Springer Nature Switzerland, 2024.

Awareness of the benefits of AI-powered training encourages learners to engage more fully with the AI tools provided, maximizing their learning outcomes and preparing them more effectively for real-world challenges. This is a simplistic breakdown of the stakeholders, in reality they will be much more nuanced and branch off within these categories.

AI-powered cybersecurity training utilizes several key technologies to enhance learner engagement and retention. Adaptive learning platforms will become increasingly popular as AI becomes more widespread. These platforms adjust the content, pace, and complexity based on real-time analysis of the learner's performance, keeping the learner in the flow state. VR and AR, which again we will discuss in more detail in Chap. 5, can simulate engaging, immersive environments where learners can experience realistic cyber threats in a controlled setting, enhancing the practical application of theoretical knowledge. Machine learning algorithms are another vessel for enhancing learner engagement and retention. These are used to analyze the effectiveness of training modules and learner performance, continuously improving the training content and delivery methods based on empirical data. Natural Language Processing (NLP) can be used to create interactive dialogues in simulations, making the learning experience more engaging and realistic. In general, leveraging these AI-driven tools, cybersecurity training becomes not just a necessity but a compelling, engaging journey that significantly enhances both the learning experience and the outcomes, equipping cybersecurity professionals with the skills and knowledge they need in an ever-changing threat landscape.

Hypothetical Scenario: Enhancing Learner Engagement with AI-Powered Cybersecurity Training

And here we are again, another hypothetical scenario wherein we can derive insights into actionable plans.

Imagine a mid-sized financial services firm, CyberSecure, which is revamping its cybersecurity training program in response to a recent surge in phishing attacks and ransomware incidents. The firm decides to implement an AI-powered cybersecurity training platform designed to enhance learner engagement and effectiveness.

Emma, a network administrator (hi again, Emma!). Emma has been with the company for 3 years and has experienced traditional cybersecurity training through seminars and static online courses. While knowledgeable, she often found previous trainings to be disengaging and not reflective of real-world scenarios she faced. The firm's new AI-driven training program aims to change this by providing a more interactive and personalized learning experience.

2.1.2.2 Implementation of AI-Powered Training

1. **Personalized Learning Paths**: The AI system begins by assessing Emma's current knowledge and skill set through a series of diagnostic tests. Based on the results, the AI identifies that while Emma is proficient in basic network security, she lacks advanced knowledge in identifying and mitigating sophisticated phishing schemes.
2. **Interactive Modules**: The AI customizes Emma's training path to include interactive modules on advanced phishing techniques, such as spear-phishing and whaling. These modules use gamified elements where Emma must detect and respond to simulated phishing attempts in a virtual environment. Each decision she makes affects the outcome, and the AI provides immediate feedback on her choices.
3. **Adaptive Difficulty**: As Emma progresses, the AI continuously adjusts the difficulty of the simulations. When she excels at certain tasks, the scenarios become more challenging, introducing elements such as multi-layered phishing attacks that involve social engineering. If Emma struggles, the AI offers supplementary content to strengthen her understanding, such as video tutorials featuring cybersecurity experts.
4. **Engagement through Realism**: To make the training as realistic and engaging as possible, the AI integrates the latest phishing trends reported in the industry, ensuring Emma is learning to combat threats that are currently active. This real-time updating keeps the content relevant and highly applicable to her daily responsibilities.
5. **Collaborative Learning**: The AI system also introduces a collaborative module where Emma can team up with other colleagues in virtual cyber defense exercises. These team-based scenarios require communication and collective problem-solving, enhancing engagement through social interaction and collective achievement.

2.1.2.3 Scenario Progression

Over several weeks, Emma finds herself deeply engaged with the training. The interactive nature of the AI-powered modules and the relevance of the content to her daily tasks keep her motivated. The instant feedback and adaptive challenges push her to continuously improve her skills. She particularly enjoys the collaborative exercises, which break the monotony and isolation of traditional e-learning.

2.1.2.4 Outcome

Thanks to the AI-driven training, Emma not only improves her ability to identify and mitigate complex phishing attempts but also feels more connected to her role. Her increased engagement in the training translates into better retention of the material, which she soon gets to put to the test.

2.1.2.5 Real-World Application

A month after completing the training, Emma detects a sophisticated spear-phishing attack aimed at one of the company's top executives. Using the skills developed during her training, she quickly responds to and mitigates the threat, preventing a potential major data breach. Emma credits the AI-powered training for her heightened awareness and rapid response.

AI-powered cybersecurity training represents a significant evolution from traditional methods, offering a more dynamic, personalized, and effective approach to learning. The differences are profound and numerous, affecting how content is delivered, how learners engage with the material, and how outcomes are measured. Traditional training typically follows a one-size-fits-all model, delivering the same content to every learner regardless of their prior knowledge, skills, or learning preferences. This can lead to disengagement, especially for learners who find the material either too challenging or too simplistic. Also, traditional training often relies on passive learning methods, such as watching videos, reading text, or listening to lectures. These methods can make it difficult to maintain learner interest and engagement over time, particularly in fields like cybersecurity, where practical, hands-on experience is crucial. In terms of adaptivity and feedback, traditional methods offers limited feedback, which is often delayed until after tests or quizzes. The lack of immediate response can hinder the learning process, as learners do not have the opportunity to correct misunderstandings in real-time. Scaling traditional training can be resource-intensive, requiring more instructors, physical space, and materials. Accessibility is also limited by geographic location and often does not cater to remote or international learners easily. Traditional training (not to continue to berate it, BUT) lacks robust mechanisms for tracking and analyzing individual learner performance over time. It's challenging to quantify the effectiveness of training or to identify areas for improvement without extensive manual effort.

On the other hand, AI-powered training provides interactive simulations and real-time problem-solving scenarios that mimic real-world situations. Learners can engage in role-playing games, virtual reality environments, and interactive puzzles that require them to apply what they've learned in a controlled, risk-free setting. This not only makes the training more engaging but also enhances retention by allowing learners to practice and internalize cybersecurity concepts and skills. It also generates detailed data on learner performance, engagement, and progression. This data can be analyzed to gain insights into the effectiveness of training modules, identify trends in learning outcomes, and refine the training program over time. This approach not only improves the quality of the training but also helps organizations measure their return on investment in training technologies. Another mention here is that in terms of scalability and accessibility, AI-powered training easily scales to accommodate an unlimited number of learners, with no additional cost per user. It's accessible from anywhere with an internet connection, making it ideal for global organizations and remote workforces. AI systems can also update content continuously to incorporate new threats and technologies, ensuring the curriculum remains relevant across all locations.

In this hypothetical scenario, CyberSecure successfully enhances cybersecurity training engagement for employees like Emma through the implementation of AI. By personalizing learning paths, providing interactive and realistic content, and adapting to individual learning speeds, the AI system not only makes the training more engaging but also significantly more effective in preparing employees to face real-world cyber threats. This scenario exemplifies how AI can transform cybersecurity training from a mundane obligation to an engaging, continuous learning journey, empowering employees with the confidence and skills to protect their organization proactively.

2.1.3 Leveraging Learning Techniques

As established, AI-powered cybersecurity training has the potential to revolutionize the way organizations approach cybersecurity education and awareness. Leveraging key principles such as the Pareto principle, spaced repetition, interleaving technique, active learning, and the Feynman technique is key for cybersecurity training. AI can optimize the learning experience, enhance learner engagement and retention, and ultimately lead to better cybersecurity practices within organizations.

The Pareto principle, also known as the 80/20 rule, states that roughly 80% of consequences come from 20% of causes.[7] In the context of cybersecurity training, this means that focusing on the most critical and frequently encountered threats can have a disproportionately large impact on an organization's overall security posture. AI algorithms can analyze historical data, threat intelligence, and user behavior to identify the most prevalent and high-risk threats. Prioritizing these topics in training programs allows organizations to ensure that their employees are well-prepared to handle the most likely and impactful security challenges.

Spaced repetition is a learning technique that involves reviewing information at increasing intervals to optimize long-term retention.[8] AI can leverage this principle by creating personalized learning schedules for each employee based on their individual performance and knowledge retention. The AI system can track an

---

[7] Dunford, Rosie, Quanrong Su, and Ekraj Tamang. "The pareto principle." (2014).
[8] Kang, Sean HK. "Spaced repetition promotes efficient and effective learning: Policy implications for instruction." *Policy Insights from the Behavioral and Brain Sciences* 3.1 (2016): 12–19.

employee's progress and automatically adjust the frequency and difficulty of training modules to ensure that key concepts are reinforced at optimal intervals. This approach helps to combat the "forgetting curve" and ensures that critical cybersecurity knowledge remains fresh and accessible when needed.

Interleaving is a technique that involves alternating between different topics or skills during the learning process.[9] Mixing related cybersecurity concepts and scenarios enables learners to feel challenged to apply their knowledge in varied contexts, promoting deeper understanding and flexible problem-solving skills. AI can dynamically generate training content that interleaves different threat scenarios, security best practices, and real-world case studies. This approach helps employees develop a more comprehensive and adaptable understanding of cybersecurity, enabling them to respond effectively to a wide range of potential threats.

Active learning engages learners in the educational process by requiring them to actively participate, ask questions, and apply their knowledge to solve problems.[10] AI-powered cybersecurity training can facilitate active learning by presenting learners with interactive simulations, hands-on labs, and real-time feedback. For example, an AI system could generate realistic phishing emails and challenge employees to identify and report suspicious content. By providing immediate feedback and explanations, the AI helps learners internalize best practices and develop practical skills that can be applied in their daily work.

The Feynman technique is a learning method that involves explaining complex concepts in simple, easy-to-understand terms.[11] AI can employ this technique by breaking down complex cybersecurity topics into clear, concise explanations that are tailored to each learner's background and level of expertise. Using natural language processing and machine learning is used for AI to analyze an employee's questions, responses, and feedback to continuously refine its explanations and analogies. This approach ensures that learners can grasp even the most technical cybersecurity concepts, regardless of their prior knowledge or experience.

One of the key advantages of AI-powered cybersecurity training is its ability to personalize the learning experience based on individual knowledge gaps and skill deficiencies. This is done by continuously assessing learner performance and engagement. Thus, AI algorithms can identify areas where each employee needs additional support or remediation. The system can then dynamically adapt the training content, difficulty, and pacing to address these individual needs. This targeted approach ensures that every employee receives the specific guidance and support they need to excel in their cybersecurity responsibilities.

Moreover, AI can enhance learner engagement and retention by gamifying the training experience. Incorporating elements such as points, badges, leaderboards,

---

[9] Pan, Steven C. "The interleaving effect: mixing it up boosts learning." *Scientific American* 313.2 (2015).

[10] Wolff, Margaret, et al. "Not another boring lecture: engaging learners with active learning techniques." *The Journal of emergency medicine* 48.1 (2015): 85–93.

[11] Adeoye, Moses Adeleke. "From Struggle to Success: The Feynman Techniques' Revolutionary Impact on Slow Learners." *Thinking Skills and Creativity Journal* 6.2 (2023).

and rewards, AI-powered training platforms can motivate employees to actively participate and strive for continuous improvement. Gamification taps into the innate human desire for competition, achievement, and recognition, making the learning process more enjoyable and engaging.[12] This will be discussed in more detail in subsequent chapters. As a result, employees are more likely to remain committed to their cybersecurity education and to apply their newly acquired knowledge and skills on the job.

Consequently, AI-powered cybersecurity training has the potential to transform the way organizations approach cybersecurity education and awareness. Using proven learning principles such as the Pareto principle, spaced repetition, interleaving, active learning, and the Feynman technique, AI can create personalized, engaging, and effective training experiences that drive positive learner outcomes. Moreover, through continuous assessment and adaptation, AI can identify and address individual knowledge gaps and skill deficiencies, ensuring that every employee receives the targeted support they need to become a strong link in the organization's cybersecurity defense. As cyber threats continue to evolve and escalate, AI-powered training will play an increasingly critical role in empowering employees with the knowledge and skills necessary in today's cyber and threat landscape.

2.1.3.1 Hypothetical Scenario: Leveraging Learning Principles

It's time for Emma to make her appearance once more. Hi, Emma.

Emma, a new hire at Cybersecure, was excited to start her role as a marketing coordinator. During her onboarding, she was introduced to the company's AI-powered cybersecurity training platform. The AI analyzed the most common and impactful threats faced by the organization (Pareto principle) and prioritized training modules accordingly.

As Emma progressed through the training, the AI used spaced repetition to reinforce key concepts. After completing a module on identifying phishing emails, the system scheduled periodic reviews at increasing intervals to ensure long-term retention. The AI also interleaved related topics, such as social engineering tactics and safe browsing habits, to help Emma develop a comprehensive understanding of cybersecurity best practices.

The training platform engaged Emma through active learning, presenting her with interactive simulations and real-world scenarios. In one module, Emma was challenged to identify and report a simulated phishing email. The AI provided immediate feedback on her performance, explaining the red flags she should have noticed and praising her for the indicators she correctly identified. When Emma struggled with technical concepts like encryption and two-factor authentication, the

---

[12] van Steen, Tommy, and Julia RA Deeleman. "Successful gamification of cybersecurity training." *Cyberpsychology, Behavior, and Social Networking* 24.9 (2021): 593–598.

AI employed the Feynman technique to break down the topics into simple, relatable explanations. Thus, analyzing Emma's questions and responses, the AI-powered cyber training platform continually refined its explanations, ensuring that she could grasp even the most complex cybersecurity principles.

As Emma continued her training, the AI monitored her performance and engagement to identify areas where she needed additional support. Noticing that Emma consistently struggled with identifying social engineering tactics, the AI adjusted her training plan to provide more focused content and practice scenarios in this area. This personalized approach helped Emma overcome her knowledge gaps and build confidence in her ability to detect and respond to social engineering attempts. To keep Emma motivated and engaged, the AI gamified her learning experience. She earned points and badges for completing modules, participating in simulated scenarios, and demonstrating knowledge retention. Emma could track her progress on a leaderboard and compare her achievements with her colleagues, fostering a sense of friendly competition and encouraging her to strive for excellence.

Over time, Emma's cybersecurity knowledge and skills grew significantly. She became adept at identifying and reporting potential threats, and she consistently applied best practices in her daily work. When Cybersecure conducted a simulated phishing campaign to test employee vigilance, Emma was among the first to report the suspicious email, demonstrating the effectiveness of her AI-powered training.

Thanks to the AI-driven cybersecurity training platform, Emma and her colleagues at Cybersecure were well-prepared to face the ever-evolving landscape of cyber threats. The personalized, engaging, and adaptive learning experience ensured that each employee had the knowledge and skills necessary to serve as a strong line of defense against potential attacks, ultimately strengthening the organization's overall cybersecurity posture.

2.2 Implementing AI-Driven Personalized Learning

This all sounds great, right? But, how can we further address how to take the theoretical into something that is actionable?

In the cybersecurity field, the gap between conceptual knowledge and practical application can be vast.[13] AI-driven personalized learning systems are uniquely positioned to bridge this gap, providing tailored learning experiences that incorporate both theoretical understanding and practical skills. Implementing such systems requires careful consideration and planning to ensure they meet the specific needs of different organizations and learners. This section outlines a framework for successfully integrating AI-driven personalized learning into cybersecurity training

---

[13] Sallos, Mark Paul, et al. "Strategy and organisational cybersecurity: a knowledge-problem perspective." *Journal of Intellectual Capital* 20.4 (2019): 581–597.

programs. This section will focus on creating a framework that can assist organizations to be able to implement their own AI-driven cybersecurity training programs.

2.2.1 Defining Goals and Objectives

Organizations must first define what they aim to achieve with AI-driven personalized learning. Goals can range from improving response times to cyber incidents, reducing the number of successful phishing attacks, or simply ensuring that all employees meet a certain baseline of cybersecurity knowledge. These goals should be specific, measurable, achievable, relevant, and time-bound (SMART).[14]

From there, an assessment of current training needs to be done. Evaluate the current cybersecurity training programs to identify strengths, weaknesses, and gaps. This assessment will help in understanding the specific needs of the organization and how AI can enhance or replace existing training modules.

Adequate technological infrastructure is essential. This includes software for managing and delivering personalized content, as well as hardware that can support sophisticated AI algorithms and data analysis. Plus, implementing AI requires handling sensitive personal and organizational data. It is crucial to ensure that data privacy laws are adhered to and that the system is secure against potential cyber threats.

The AI system should be scalable and flexible to accommodate the growing or changing needs of the organization. It should be capable of serving different numbers of users and adapt to various cybersecurity scenarios. For seamless functionality, the AI-driven learning platform needs to integrate well with existing LMS (Learning Management Systems) and other educational tools. This ensures that learners have a cohesive experience and that administrators can track progress comprehensively.

2.2.2 Creating a Roadmap for Different Organizations

In larger settings, AI-driven personalized learning can be implemented at scale to cover extensive employee bases across multiple locations. It's vital to have a centralized management system and robust server capabilities to handle the increased load. In contrast, smaller organizations should focus on cost-effective AI solutions that offer the most essential features without extensive customization, to keep the implementation practical and manageable.

---

[14] Bjerke, May Britt, and Ralph Renger. "Being smart about writing SMART objectives." *Evaluation and program planning* 61 (2017): 125–127.

Depending on the industry, cybersecurity threats can vary significantly. Personalized learning in healthcare, for instance, should emphasize compliance and patient data protection, whereas in finance, the focus might be on transaction security and fraud prevention. Furthermore, the training approach must align with the organizational culture. Organizations that promote self-directed learning would benefit from AI systems that provide learners with more control over their learning paths, whereas more hierarchical organizations might prefer a more structured approach.

2.2.3 Making It Actionable

To turn this framework into an actionable plan, organizations and individuals should:

1. Start with a pilot program focusing on a specific department or learning goal to measure the effectiveness.
2. Gradually expand the program while continuously monitoring and adjusting the approach based on feedback and learning outcomes.
3. Provide ongoing support and training for users to maximize their engagement and success with the AI learning tools.

This framework is meant to be high level and adaptable regardless of the size, industry, or culture of the organization.

Let's not forget about implementation for individual learners. What if you are someone that is interested in the cybersecurity field or someone that is looking to enter it? Or what if you are someone that has been seeing a lot of scary thinsg in the news about how you and your data could be potentially breached and you want to know how to protect yourselves, your families and your communities?

2.2.4 Implementation for Individual Learners

Individuals seeking to enter the cybersecurity field can also leverage AI-driven personalized learning. First, choose a learning platform that offers courses in cybersecurity and supports personalized learning paths. Then, set some goals. Define what areas of cybersecurity are most relevant to your career goals and use AI tools to create a personalized learning plan. Consistency is key in learning. Regular interaction with the AI system ensures steady progress and retention of knowledge.

2.2.5 Assessing Learner Profiles and Competencies

Based on the framework created in Sect. 2.2, we start off by defining goals and objectives. Within the realm of that, especially when creating cybersecurity training that is personalized for learners, organizations have to see what these learner profiles are and their current competencies. Assessing learner profiles and competencies is a crucial first step in implementing AI-driven personalized learning in cybersecurity training.[15] This process ensures that the training content is not only relevant but also tailored to the specific needs and abilities of each learner. Understanding and defining these profiles allow organizations to create highly effective and engaging learning paths, enhancing both the efficiency and the effectiveness of their cybersecurity training efforts. In the broader framework of AI-powered personalized learning, assessing learner profiles and competencies serves as the foundation upon which all other elements are built. This assessment informs the customization of content, the complexity of tasks, and the method of delivery, ensuring that each aspect of the training is optimized for the individual learner.

There are different ways to measure learner profiles and competencies—so how do you measure them?

1. Initial Diagnostic Assessments: Before starting the training, conduct assessments to gauge the existing knowledge and skill levels of the learners. This can include standardized tests, quizzes, or practical tasks that cover a broad range of cybersecurity topics.
2. Ongoing Monitoring: Utilize AI to continuously monitor learner performance throughout the training. AI can analyze responses, track progress, and even measure the time taken to complete tasks to adjust the difficulty and focus of the training accordingly.
3. Feedback Mechanisms: Implement systems that allow learners to provide feedback on the training content. This can help in understanding learner preferences, difficulties they are encountering, and the overall satisfaction with the training.[16]

For the assessment to be effective, there are other considerations that need to be made.

1. Define What Needs to Be Assessed: Determine which competencies are critical for your organization's cybersecurity needs. This could range from basic security practices to advanced threat detection and mitigation strategies depending on the roles of the learners.

---

[15] Jawhar, Shadi, Jeremy Miller, and Zeina Bitar. "AI-Driven Customized Cyber Security Training and Awareness." *2024 IEEE 3rd International Conference on AI in Cybersecurity (ICAIC)*. IEEE, 2024.

[16] Švábenský, V. *Automated feedback for cybersecurity training*. Diss. Doctoral thesis, Masaryk University, 2022. [Online]. Available: https://is.muni.cz/th/dg3b4, 2022.

2. Consider the Diversity of the Workforce: Take into account the varied backgrounds and roles of the workforce. A one-size-fits-all assessment approach might not be effective for diverse groups, so consider role-specific and skill-level-specific assessments to accurately measure competencies.
3. Privacy and Ethical Considerations: Ensure that the assessment processes respect learner privacy and adhere to ethical guidelines. It's crucial to maintain transparency about how data from assessments will be used and to secure consent from the learners. Think of data privacy legislation that we see—like the General Data Protection Regulation (GDPR) and the California Consumer Privacy Act (CCPA). In our evolving regulatory landscape, data minimization privacy laws are also an important factor to consider, like the Maryland Online Data Privacy Act of 2024 (MODPA).[17] These are important considerations to factor in when collecting, interacting, and storing data that is sensitive, and learner profiles and their skill levels are absolutely sensitive information.

Assessing learner profiles and competencies is a fundamental aspect of implementing AI-driven personalized learning in cybersecurity training. Effectively measuring these parameters, allows organizations to ensure that their training programs are not just comprehensive but also highly. This initial step not only sets the stage for a successful personalized learning experience but also helps in building a robust cybersecurity posture tailored to the specific needs and capabilities of the organization's workforce.

2.2.6 Designing Adaptive Learning Paths and Content

After assessing learner profiles and competencies, the next crucial step for organizations is to design adaptive learning paths and content that cater specifically to the needs of their workforce. This involves crafting educational programs that adjust in real-time to the skill levels and learning progress of individuals, ensuring that every learner remains engaged, challenged, and effectively educated.

Step 1: Define Learning Objectives Based on Assessed Needs Start by translating the data gathered from assessing learner profiles and competencies into specific learning objectives. These should align with both individual growth needs and organizational cybersecurity goals. Questions to consider include:

- What are the critical skills and knowledge areas where gaps were identified?
- How do these gaps align with the broader cybersecurity risks the organization faces?

---

[17] Maryland General Assembly. https://mgaleg.maryland.gov/mgawebsite/Legislation/Details/sb0541

2.2 Implementing AI-Driven Personalized Learning

Step 2: Segment Learning into Modular Components[18] Break down the cybersecurity training into modular components that can be rearranged or adjusted according to the needs of the learner. Each module should focus on a specific skill or knowledge area, ranging from basic cybersecurity awareness for all employees to advanced threat detection techniques for IT staff.

Step 3: Develop Adaptive Frameworks Utilize an AI-driven LMS (Learning Management System) that supports adaptivity. This system should be able to:

- Automatically adjust the difficulty level of tasks based on real-time performance data.
- Provide branching scenarios that allow learners to take different paths through content based on their responses and choices.
- Offer personalized feedback and recommend additional resources when necessary.

Step 4: Implement Continuous Feedback Loops Incorporate mechanisms for continuous feedback within the learning path, both from the learners and the AI system. This feedback is crucial for refining the learning experience and ensuring that the content remains relevant and engaging.

2.2.6.1 Designing the Content

Content Formats Decide on a variety of content formats to cater to different learning styles and enhance engagement. These can include:

- Interactive simulations for hands-on practice.
- Video tutorials for visual and auditory learners.
- Infographics and cheat sheets for quick reference and revision.
- Gamified elements, such as quizzes and leaderboards, to motivate and engage learners.

Let's delve deeper into How the aforementioned could incorporate AI.

Customization for Cybersecurity Training and Awareness For cybersecurity training, ensure that the content covers both technical skills and broader awareness:

- Technical Training: Use simulations and virtual labs that allow employees to practice in a safe, controlled environment. For example, setting up firewalls, detecting network intrusions, or responding to simulated phishing attacks.
- Awareness Training: Focus on creating content that highlights the importance of cybersecurity in everyday activities. This could include recognizing phishing emails, the importance of strong passwords, and secure internet practices.

---

[18] Hatzivasilis, George, et al. "Modern aspects of cyber-security training and continuous adaptation of programmes to trainees." *Applied Sciences* 10.16 (2020): 5702.

Creating Cyber Ranges[19] Cyber ranges provide a dynamic platform for cybersecurity training, where professionals can engage in simulated cybersecurity scenarios that mimic real-world challenges. To design a cyber range that supports adaptive learning:

- Develop Scenarios Based on Real-World Threats: Use recent cybersecurity incidents as templates to create realistic training scenarios.
- Incorporate Branching Paths: Allow different responses to lead to different outcomes, simulating the unpredictability of real cybersecurity threats.
- Use AI to Adjust Scenarios in Real Time: Depending on the learner's actions and decisions, the AI should modify the scenario difficulty and complexity, providing a truly adaptive learning environment.

Actionable Steps for Organizations

1. Invest in AI-Enabled Learning Technologies: Ensure that your LMS or training platform can support adaptive learning paths and content delivery.
2. Train Your Trainers: Equip your trainers with the skills to use AI tools effectively and to interpret data from AI assessments to better support learners.
3. Regularly Update Content: Cybersecurity is a fast-evolving field. Regular updates to training content are necessary to keep the training relevant.
4. Evaluate and Iterate: Continuously measure the effectiveness of training programs and make adjustments based on learner performance and feedback.

Implementation

Implementing AI in cybersecurity training to effectively address individual knowledge gaps and skill deficiencies involves strategic planning and careful consideration at various levels of an organization.

Hypothetical Example: CyberSecure's AI-Powered Cybersecurity Training and Awareness Program

Well, it's that time again. Let's go through a hypothetical example of an organization that looks to revolutionize its cybersecurity training practices to incorporate AI.

Background CyberSecure, a multinational corporation specializing in data protection services, recognizes the escalating cyber threats and acknowledges that comprehensive cybersecurity awareness and training are crucial for all its staff. To address this, CyberSecure decides to deploy an AI-powered training program tailored to enhance both cybersecurity skills and general awareness across its diverse workforce.

---

[19] Podnar, Thomas G., et al. "Foundation of cyber ranges." *Software Engineering Institute, Pittsburgh, PA* (2021).

2.2 Implementing AI-Driven Personalized Learning

Implementation Strategy

Step 1: Assessing Learner Profiles and Competencies CyberSecure begins by conducting an organization-wide survey to assess existing cybersecurity knowledge and identify specific learning gaps. Using AI algorithms, they analyze the survey data to create detailed profiles for each employee, categorizing them by their current skill levels, roles, and learning preferences.

Step 2: Designing Adaptive Learning Paths Using the information gathered, CyberSecure designs a two-tier training program:

- **Cybersecurity Training for IT Staff**: Focused on advanced technical skills like threat analysis, incident response, and network security enhancements.
- **Cybersecurity Awareness for General Staff**: Concentrates on fundamental practices such as password management, recognizing phishing attempts, and secure internet usage.

Step 3: Developing Content Formats CyberSecure chooses several AI-enhanced content formats to cater to different learning styles:

- **Interactive Simulations**: IT staff participate in simulated cyber-attack scenarios where they must detect and mitigate threats in real-time. The AI adjusts the complexity based on their actions and decisions.
- **Video Tutorials**: Short, engaging videos explain cybersecurity basics to general staff, with interactive questions embedded by AI to ensure understanding and retention.
- **Infographics and Cheat Sheets**: Designed for quick reference, these tools are available for all staff, featuring clickable elements that provide more in-depth information on specific cybersecurity topics.
- **Gamified Elements**: Quizzes and leaderboards are introduced to make learning engaging. AI customizes quiz questions based on individual learning progress and updates leaderboards in real-time to foster a competitive learning environment.

Step 4: Implementing and Monitoring the Training Program The training is rolled out through CyberSecure's AI-enabled Learning Management System (LMS), which tracks participation, progress, and proficiency. AI analytics help CyberSecure monitor the effectiveness of the training and make adjustments where necessary.

2.2.6.2 Cyber Ranges

For the IT staff, CyberSecure sets up a cyber range where they can engage in more complex security tasks and scenarios. This adaptive learning environment allows IT professionals to explore different response strategies to cybersecurity incidents, with AI dynamically altering the scenarios based on their actions to provide a continuous challenge.

2.2.6.3 Outcome and Evaluation

After 6 months, CyberSecure reviews the training outcomes. They find a significant improvement in both the technical proficiency of their IT staff and the cybersecurity awareness among general staff. The AI's real-time feedback and adaptability have allowed employees to progress at their optimal pace and maintain high engagement levels.

The program's success leads to a decision to schedule bi-annual review sessions to update the training content based on the latest cyber threat landscapes and emerging technologies. CyberSecure plans to expand this training approach to include their international branches, adapting the content to regional cybersecurity challenges and compliance requirements. This comprehensive approach ensures that all staff, regardless of their role, are equipped with the necessary knowledge and skills to contribute to the organization's overall cyber resilience.

2.2.7 *Monitoring and Optimizing Learning Outcomes*

Monitoring and optimizing learning outcomes are critical processes in ensuring the effectiveness of AI-powered cybersecurity training programs. These processes enable organizations to assess the efficacy of training, identify areas for improvement, and adjust training strategies to meet evolving needs. Organizations can gain a comprehensive understanding of how well the training meets its objectives and how it could be enhanced by using both qualitative and quantitative metrics.

Quantitative metrics provide concrete data that informs the training's impact and areas needing adjustment.[20] Completion rates, for instance, help gauge overall engagement and pinpoint potential barriers within the training content that might be causing learners to drop off. Pre- and post-training assessments are used to measure knowledge gains and identify specific competencies where learners are either struggling or excelling. Additionally, performance metrics from AI-powered simulations and gamified environments—such as decision accuracy, response times, and outcomes—offer in-depth insights into how well learners are developing necessary skills. Engagement metrics also play a key role, tracking how frequently and for how long users interact with the training materials, which helps in identifying when and where learners disengage, possibly indicating content that may be overly complex or insufficiently challenging.

On the qualitative side, various methods help capture the nuanced feedback and experiences of the participants, providing context to the numbers derived from quantitative data.[21] Surveys and feedback forms solicit regular input from learners

---

[20] Salas, Eduardo, et al. "Performance measurement in simulation-based training: A review and best practices." *Simulation in Aviation Training* (2017): 393–441.

[21] Tracy, Sarah J. *Qualitative research methods: Collecting evidence, crafting analysis, communicating impact.* John Wiley & Sons, 2019.

about the training's relevance, usability, and how engaging they find the material, shedding light on aspects that quantitative metrics might miss. Focus groups allow for deeper exploration into learners' experiences, challenges faced, and their perceptions of the training program, offering rich, detailed feedback that can guide further refinement of the training content. Observational studies, where trainers or researchers watch how participants interact with the training in real-time, can yield valuable insights into the practical engagement and interactivity of the training environment. Together, these qualitative assessments help ensure the training not only meets learning objectives but is also well-received and effectively engages participants, enhancing the overall learning experience.

Using both quantitative and qualitative metrics is crucial because it allows organizations to gather a wide range of data. Quantitative data provides hard numbers that are essential for measuring direct outcomes and benchmarking progress against objectives. Qualitative data, on the other hand, offers context and deeper insights into the numbers, such as why certain modules might have low engagement or why some learners are not achieving learning goals. This mixed-methods approach ensures that training programs are not only effective in terms of measurable results but also relevant and genuinely beneficial to participants.

2.2.7.1 Using AI to Monitor and Optimize Learning Outcomes

AI can significantly enhance the monitoring of learning outcomes through real-time data analysis and adaptive learning technologies.[22] AI systems can automatically adjust the difficulty of training materials based on the learner's performance, ensuring that each participant is challenged appropriately. Moreover, AI can analyze large datasets from learner interactions to identify patterns and trends that may not be visible to human trainers. For example, if many participants are consistently making similar errors in a particular simulation scenario, the AI can flag this as an area for content improvement. AI also supports the personalization of learning paths by continuously updating training models based on individual and group performance data. This ensures that the training remains relevant and effectively addresses the specific needs of each learner.

Once organizations have collected and analyzed data from their training programs, they can harness these insights to refine and optimize the effectiveness of their training initiatives. By leveraging AI analytics, training content can be meticulously tailored to better meet the specific needs of the workforce. This includes simplifying complex topics for broader understanding and providing additional resources or targeted training modules to address areas where performance metrics indicate underperformance. Additionally, insights derived from engagement metrics can be instrumental in enhancing the interactivity of the training materials. For

---

[22] Kabudi, Tumaini, Ilias Pappas, and Dag Håkon Olsen. "AI-enabled adaptive learning systems: A systematic mapping of the literature." *Computers and Education: Artificial Intelligence* 2 (2021): 100017.

example, organizations can develop more engaging content formats like realistic simulations or gamified elements that not only mirror real-world scenarios but also boost learner participation and motivation.

Furthermore, AI plays a pivotal role in personalizing learning at scale, enabling the customization of training content across various organizational roles, from entry-level positions to senior management. This ensures that every staff member receives training that is not only relevant to their specific duties but also aligned with their individual learning progress and needs. Subsequently, integrating these strategies, organizations can significantly enhance the effectiveness, relevance, and engagement of their cybersecurity training programs, fostering a more knowledgeable and prepared workforce.

Senior leaders can effectively leverage AI-generated insights to continuously enhance training outcomes through strategic adjustments and feedback loops.[23] Thus, by analyzing reports produced by AI, leaders can make informed decisions about where to allocate training resources effectively to maximize returns. Furthermore, fostering a culture where end-users are encouraged to provide feedback on the training content can establish a valuable feedback loop. This feedback loop allows for the training to evolve dynamically based on direct user input, significantly enhancing its relevance and effectiveness. Integrating AI into both the delivery and evaluation of cybersecurity training allows organizations to not only monitor but also continuously improve their programs. This proactive approach ensures that the training keeps pace with the rapidly evolving field of cybersecurity and is attuned to the specific and changing needs of the organization and its workforce.

Hypothetical Example: Leveraging AI to Monitor & Optimize Learner Outcomes

In theory, this sounds great. Let's go through a practical example of how organizations can leverage AI to monitor and optimize learner outcomes of AI-powered cybersecurity training. CyberSecure, a prominent security firm, acknowledged the vital need for robust cybersecurity training due to the sensitive nature of its operations and decided to overhaul its existing training program by integrating AI technologies. This initiative aimed to enhance the monitoring and optimization of learning outcomes, ensuring that the training remained relevant and effective.

To begin, CyberSecure established a series of quantitative and qualitative metrics to assess the effectiveness of their AI-enhanced training. Quantitatively, the firm tracked completion rates of the training sessions, where initial low rates signaled potential engagement issues or content irrelevance, prompting deeper investigation. They also conducted standardized pre- and post-training assessments to quantify knowledge gains and pinpoint areas of difficulty or success among learners.

---

[23] Jarrahi, Mohammad Hossein, et al. "Artificial intelligence: A strategy to harness its power through organizational learning." *Journal of Business Strategy* 44.3 (2023): 126–135.

Additionally, the AI-powered simulations enabled CyberSecure to monitor actions, decision accuracy, response times, and outcomes, providing insights into skill development. Engagement metrics were also scrutinized, with AI systems tracking how often and how long employees interacted with the training materials to identify disengagement points.

On the qualitative side, CyberSecure collected feedback through surveys after each training module, which offered insights into the training's relevance and engagement levels. Focus groups were held monthly to delve deeper into employees' experiences and challenges, while observational studies by trainers during the sessions provided real-time insights into how interactive and engaging the content was.

With this comprehensive monitoring setup, the AI was used to dynamically adjust the training program. AI algorithms personalized and modified the difficulty of training materials in real time based on assessment results and engagement data. This allowed for the introduction of more complex simulations for employees excelling at basic concepts and the redesign of problematic modules identified through error pattern analysis. Insights from engagement metrics also led to the development of more interactive content, such as virtual reality simulations of cybersecurity breach scenarios, which significantly increased participation and practical skill application.

From the data and insights gathered, CyberSecure was able to optimize its training outcomes effectively. AI analytics facilitated the simplification of complex topics and the provision of additional resources where needed, making the training more accessible and effective. The AI-developed gamified elements and real-world scenario simulations enhanced learner engagement and deepened the understanding of cybersecurity challenges. Additionally, AI supported the scaling of personalized learning paths across the organization, catering to various roles from entry-level to senior management.

CyberSecure's senior leaders regularly reviewed AI-generated reports to make strategic adjustments in the allocation of training resources. This ensured that the training not only remained cutting-edge in terms of content but also highly relevant and engaging for all staff members. Furthermore, by fostering a culture of continuous feedback, CyberSecure maintained a dynamic loop where training evolved based on direct user input, continuously enhancing its relevance and effectiveness.

Through this integrated approach, using both AI for delivery and evaluation, CyberSecure successfully developed a cybersecurity training program that not only kept pace with the rapidly evolving field but also met the unique and changing needs of its workforce, thereby significantly strengthening its overall cybersecurity posture.

Something to think about is how your organization can leverage AI-powered technologies to transform and personalize cybersecurity training, ensuring it is not only effective but also engaging for every level of employee? What steps will you take to implement such innovations and continuously adapt to the evolving cybersecurity landscape?

References

1. Pratama, M. P., Sampelolo, R., & Lura, H. (2023). Revolutionizing education: Harnessing the power of artificial intelligence for personalized learning. *Klasikal: Journal of Education, Language Teaching and Science, 5*(2), 350–357.
2. Chang, J., & Xu, L. (2019). The study on students' participation in personalized learning under the background of artificial intelligence. In *2019 10th international conference on information Technology in Medicine and Education (ITME)*. IEEE.
3. Pavlas, D., et al. (2010). Game-based learning: The impact of flow state and videogame self-efficacy. In *Proceedings of the human factors and ergonomics society annual meeting* (Vol. 54. No. 28). Sage.
4. Alnajim, A. M., et al. (2023). Exploring cybersecurity education and training techniques: A comprehensive review of traditional, virtual reality, and augmented reality approaches. *Symmetry, 15*(12), 2175.
5. Al-Daeef, M. (2022). Challenges of the success of cybersecurity training programs. *Journal of Basic Sciences, 35*(2), 27–36.
6. Prümmer, J. (2024). The role of cognition in developing successful cybersecurity training programs–passive vs. active engagement. In *International Conference on Human-Computer Interaction*. Springer.
7. Dunford, R., Su, Q., & Tamang, E. (2014). *The Pareto principle*.
8. Kang, S. H. K. (2016). Spaced repetition promotes efficient and effective learning: Policy implications for instruction. *Policy Insights from the Behavioral and Brain Sciences, 3*(1), 12–19.
9. Pan, S. C. (2015). The interleaving effect: Mixing it up boosts learning. *Scientific American, 313*, 2.
10. Wolff, M., et al. (2015). Not another boring lecture: Engaging learners with active learning techniques. *The Journal of Emergency Medicine, 48*(1), 85–93.
11. Adeoye, M. A. (2023). From struggle to success: The Feynman Techniques' revolutionary impact on slow learners. *Thinking Skills and Creativity Journal, 6*, 2.
12. van Steen, T., & Deeleman, J. R. A. (2021). Successful gamification of cybersecurity training. *Cyberpsychology, Behavior, and Social Networking, 24*(9), 593–598.
13. Sallos, M. P., et al. (2019). Strategy and organisational cybersecurity: A knowledge-problem perspective. *Journal of Intellectual Capital, 20*(4), 581–597.
14. Bjerke, M. B., & Renger, R. (2017). Being SMART about writing SMART objectives. *Evaluation and Program Planning, 61*, 125–127.
15. Jawhar, S., Miller, J., & Bitar, Z. (2024). AI-driven customized cyber security training and awareness. In *2024 IEEE 3rd international conference on AI in cybersecurity (ICAIC)*. IEEE.
16. Švábenský, V. (2022). *Automated feedback for cybersecurity training*. Dissertation, Doctoral thesis, Masaryk University [Online]. Available: https://is.muni.cz/th/dg3b4
17. Maryland Online Data Privacy Act of 2024. Maryland General Assembly. https://mgaleg.maryland.gov/mgawebsite/Legislation/Details/sb0541
18. Hatzivasilis, G., et al. (2020). Modern aspects of cyber-security training and continuous adaptation of programmes to trainees. *Applied Sciences, 10*(16), 5702.
19. Podnar, T. G., et al. (2021). *Foundation of cyber ranges*. Software Engineering Institute.
20. Salas, E., et al. (2017). Performance measurement in simulation-based training: A review and best practices. *Simulation in Aviation Training*, 393–441.
21. Tracy, S. J. (2019). *Qualitative research methods: Collecting evidence, crafting analysis, communicating impact*. Wiley.
22. Kabudi, T., Pappas, I., & Olsen, D. H. (2021). AI-enabled adaptive learning systems: A systematic mapping of the literature. *Computers and Education: Artificial Intelligence, 2*, 100017.
23. Jarrahi, M. H., et al. (2023). Artificial intelligence: A strategy to harness its power through organizational learning. *Journal of Business Strategy, 44*(3), 126–135.

Chapter 3
Gamification and Immersive Learning with AI

Traditional approaches to cybersecurity training are being rapidly outpaced by more engaging, innovative methods facilitated by advancements in artificial intelligence. Chapter 3 of this book delves deep into the transformative power of AI in crafting game-like training experiences that not only captivate but also educate. Through a blend of gamification and immersive learning techniques, AI is redefining how cybersecurity training is conducted. Consequently, making it more interactive, enjoyable, and effective.

This chapter explores the dynamic role of gamification in cybersecurity training, illustrating how leveraging elements such as intrinsic and extrinsic rewards, competitive leaderboards, badges, and narrative storytelling can significantly enhance learner motivation and engagement. These elements promote active learning and skill acquisition by incorporating interactive simulations and scenarios that provide immediate feedback and reinforcement, support gradual skill progression, and foster collaborative learning through social interaction.

Further, the discussion extends into AI-powered immersive learning experiences that employ realistic threat scenarios and simulations. These experiences are tailored to the learner's skill level and progress, offering a controlled environment to practice responses to a wide range of cybersecurity challenges. Integration of real-world threat intelligence ensures that the training remains relevant and up-to-date, continuously adapting to the latest cyber threats and trends.

The chapter also covers the application of virtual reality (VR) and augmented reality (AR) in creating immersive cybersecurity training environments. This chapter will briefly go over these concepts; however, Chap. 5 delves deeper into the intersection of VR/AR training modules and AI. In general, these technologies provide hands-on interaction with simulated tools and systems, enhancing situational awareness and critical decision-making skills under stress. Additionally, the balance between educational value and entertainment is scrutinized to ensure that the training not only engages but also effectively conveys critical knowledge and skills.

Overall, the goal of this chapter is to offer valuable insights into how organizations can leverage these technologies to create highly effective, engaging, and adaptive cybersecurity training programs. The ultimate goal is to prepare learners not just to respond to current threats but also to adapt to the evolving landscape of cybersecurity challenges.

3.1 The Power of Gamification in Cybersecurity Training

Section 3.1 delves into the dynamic world of gamification and its transformative impact on cybersecurity training. Gamification, which integrates game-design elements into learning, proves to be an exceptional strategy to increase learner motivation and engagement. This section explores various facets of gamification including intrinsic and extrinsic rewards that encourage personal satisfaction and tangible rewards, respectively. It also examines how leaderboards and competitive elements can invoke a spirit of competition and drive performance among learners. Additionally, the use of badges, points, and achievements provides tangible milestones in the learning journey, while narrative and storytelling embed complex cybersecurity concepts into relatable and engaging contexts.

Furthermore, gamification plays a crucial role in promoting active learning and skill acquisition. This segment of the chapter discusses how interactive simulations and scenarios allow learners to practice real-world applications in a risk-free environment, enhancing both understanding and retention. Immediate feedback and reinforcement help correct mistakes in real-time, solidifying learning and boosting confidence. Gradual skill progression and mastery are facilitated through structured difficulty levels that ensure continuous learning without overwhelming the students. Lastly, collaborative learning and social interaction are emphasized, showcasing how gamified learning can foster teamwork and communication skills among learners, critical components in the cybersecurity field. This comprehensive approach not only makes learning more enjoyable but also more effective, equipping learners with the skills and knowledge necessary to face real-world cybersecurity challenges.

3.1.1 Increasing Learner Motivation and Engagement

In the realm of AI-powered cybersecurity training, effectively leveraging both intrinsic and extrinsic rewards is crucial for enhancing learner motivation and engagement.[1] Intrinsic rewards stem from the internal satisfaction and personal joy

---

[1] Sharma, Rajesh, and Sunita Thapa. "Cybersecurity awareness, education, and behavioral change: strategies for promoting secure online practices among end users." *Eigenpub Review of Science and Technology* 7.1 (2023): 224–238.

of learning.[2] These are particularly significant as they tap into the learner's psychological need for growth and achievement. AI systems enhance this experience by customizing challenges to precisely match each learner's skill level, ensuring that every module or task provides a sense of accomplishment. As learners progress and overcome tailored challenges, their intrinsic motivation increases due to the personal satisfaction gained from mastering new skills.

On the flip side, extrinsic rewards[3] like certificates, public recognition, or tangible prizes play a complementary role. AI systems are adept at managing and distributing these rewards, making decisions based on the achievement of predefined criteria. These rewards are crucial for keeping learners engaged, especially in a field as demanding as cybersecurity, where continuous learning and up-to-date knowledge are imperative. Thus, offering these extrinsic motivators, organizations can spur learners to engage more deeply with the training content, aiming to achieve specific milestones that yield tangible rewards.

However, implementing a reward system that balances intrinsic and extrinsic factors presents challenges. The key issue lies in designing a system that motivates effectively without leading to undue competition or stress among learners. It's essential for organizations to ensure that these rewards are seen as fair and attainable and that they directly correlate with the desired learning outcomes. This balance is vital to prevent any negative feelings or competitive tensions that could detract from the learning experience.

Organizations must therefore approach the design of these reward systems with care and precision. Ensuring fairness and maintaining alignment with educational goals are crucial aspects that require attention. Consequently, by doing so, organizations can create a learning environment where rewards foster a positive and productive atmosphere. This thoughtful approach ensures that both types of rewards— intrinsic and extrinsic—serve their purpose of encouraging continuous engagement and improvement, thereby enriching the overall effectiveness of cybersecurity training programs.

Imagine an AI-powered cybersecurity training scenario designed for a large tech company, where each employee embarks on a personalized learning journey tailored by AI. As learners progress through modules, AI dynamically adjusts the difficulty based on their performance, ensuring that tasks are neither too easy nor overly challenging. For instance, an employee who excels at identifying phishing attempts may receive more complex simulations involving sophisticated social engineering tactics, enhancing their intrinsic motivation through tailored challenges that promote a sense of personal achievement. Simultaneously, the AI system tracks each learner's achievements, awarding digital badges and certificates for milestones reached, such as completing a difficult module or contributing to a team project in a

---

[2] Kam, Hwee-Joo, et al. "Cultivating cybersecurity learning: An integration of self-determination and flow." *Computers & Security* 96 (2020): 101875.

[3] Lee, Daeun, Harjinder Singh Lallie, and Nadine Michaelides. "The impact of an employee's psychological contract breach on compliance with information security policies: intrinsic and extrinsic motivation." *Cognition, Technology & Work* 25.2 (2023): 273–289.

simulated environment. These rewards are displayed on a public leaderboard, fostering a healthy competitive atmosphere within the workplace. This dual approach of personal growth (intrinsic) and recognition (extrinsic) not only keeps the training engaging but also closely aligns with the organization's goals of developing a highly skilled cybersecurity workforce.

3.1.1.1 Leaderboards and Competitive Elements

Incorporating leaderboards and competitive elements into cybersecurity training programs can significantly enhance learner motivation and engagement by leveraging natural human competitiveness.[4] These features tap into the desire to outperform peers and provide a clear, visible measure of progress and achievement. When learners see their names rise on leaderboards, it not only validates their effort and skill but also motivates them to engage more deeply with the content to maintain or improve their ranking.

The primary benefit of integrating leaderboards and competitive elements is increased engagement. Turning learning into a competitive activity, organizations can drive participants to dedicate more time and effort to their training. This competitive framework encourages continuous interaction with the training material, which can lead to better retention of information and a deeper understanding of complex cybersecurity concepts. Furthermore, competition can foster a sense of community and camaraderie among participants, as they engage not only in personal achievement but also in group dynamics and team-based challenges.

Leaderboards and competitive elements can serve as powerful motivational tools.[5] They provide continuous feedback, allowing learners to see how they rank in relation to their peers and what they need to do to improve. This ongoing feedback loop can help maintain high levels of motivation throughout the training program. Additionally, for organizations that choose to reward top performers with prizes or public recognition, these competitive elements can offer additional incentives for learners to engage with and excel in their training.

However, the incorporation of competitive elements does not come without challenges and potential downsides. For some individuals, competitive environments can lead to stress and anxiety, which might detract from the learning experience rather than enhance it. High levels of competition may also foster a win-at-all-costs attitude that could encourage unethical behavior, such as cheating or sabotage. Moreover, not all learners are motivated by competition; some may prefer collaborative or self-paced learning environments and could feel alienated or demotivated

---

[4] Malone, Mac, et al. "To gamify or not? on leaderboard effects, student engagement and learning outcomes in a cybersecurity intervention." *Proceedings of the 52nd ACM Technical Symposium on Computer Science Education*. 2021.

[5] Balon, Tyler, and Ibrahim Baggili. "Cybercompetitions: A survey of competitions, tools, and systems to support cybersecurity education." *Education and Information Technologies* 28.9 (2023): 11759–11,791.

by a competitive format. There's also the risk that competition might create a hostile or overly competitive workplace culture, which can be counterproductive. It's crucial for organizations to consider their specific culture and the personalities of their employees when designing these systems. The goal is to use competition to motivate and engage, not to demoralize or divide.

The effectiveness of leaderboards and competitive elements largely depends on the organization's culture and the design of the competition. It is essential for these elements to be implemented in a way that aligns with the organization's values and the nature of its workforce. For example, an organization that values collaboration over competition might find that leaderboards need to be carefully balanced with team-based achievements and rewards that promote group success rather than individual glory.

AI can significantly enhance the effectiveness and appeal of leaderboards and competitive elements in cybersecurity training programs. Consequently, automating the tracking and updating of leaderboards, AI ensures that performance metrics are accurately and promptly reflected, allowing participants to see their rankings change in real-time as they progress through the training. This immediate feedback can motivate learners to deepen their engagement with the material, striving to improve their performance and ranking. Furthermore, AI can personalize challenges based on individual performance data, ensuring that all participants, regardless of their initial skill level, find the competitions stimulating yet achievable.

However, while AI facilitates a dynamic and responsive competitive environment, organizations must navigate potential challenges carefully. The pressure of continuous competition can lead to stress or counterproductive behaviors among participants.[6] Therefore, AI systems can also be programmed to moderate the competitive aspects by providing periodic encouragement and constructive feedback, rather than just ranking updates. This approach helps to maintain motivation and prevents the negative aspects of competition from overshadowing the learning experience. Additionally, AI can help tailor the competitive framework to fit the organizational culture, perhaps by emphasizing team-based competitions or integrating collaborative challenges where teamwork leads to shared rewards.

3.1.1.2 Badges, Points, and Achievements

Offering badges, points, and achievements in cybersecurity training programs serves as a compelling motivational strategy, engaging learners by marking their progress and accomplishments. This system of rewards caters to the human desire for recognition and achievement, providing tangible evidence of one's learning and mastery over time. Unlike leaderboards, which foster a competitive environment, badges and points focus on personal achievement, making them suitable for a wider

---

[6] Mclaughlin, Kevin. *A Quantitative Study of Learner Choice in Cybersecurity Training: Do They Even Want Gamification?*. Diss. Colorado Technical University, 2023.

range of organizational cultures, particularly those that emphasize individual growth and development over competition.

The introduction of badges, points, and achievements in training programs can significantly enhance learner engagement by providing clear goals and rewards for reaching them. These rewards help to break down the training content into smaller, manageable tasks, which can make the learning process feel less daunting and more achievable. Each badge or point earned acts as a milestone that learners can look back on to see how far they have come, boosting their morale and motivating them to continue progressing. Furthermore, this system allows learners to take pride in their accomplishments, which can be particularly motivating in fields like cybersecurity, where the complexity and ever-changing nature of the content can otherwise be overwhelming. For organizations, implementing a system of badges, points, and achievements can help standardize training outcomes by clearly defining what constitutes success in various stages of the training. This clarity can aid in the overall management of the training program, ensuring that all learners are meeting the desired standards and objectives.

While badges and achievements offer many benefits, there are challenges to consider. It's essential to design these rewards so that they are meaningful and genuinely reflective of significant accomplishments. There is a risk of "badge inflation," where too many badges are awarded too easily, diminishing their value and impact on motivation. Additionally, not all learners are motivated by the same types of rewards, and some may find a system that focuses heavily on badges and points to be trivial or patronizing. The effectiveness of this system can also depend heavily on an organization's culture. In environments where personal achievement and self-improvement are valued, badges and achievements can reinforce the organization's cultural norms and contribute positively to employee engagement. Conversely, in settings where external rewards are seen as less important, or where intrinsic motivation is more heavily emphasized, the impact of badges and points might be minimal.

AI technology can be uniquely positioned to enhance the effectiveness of badges, points, and achievements in cybersecurity training. AI, through analyzing learner data, can help to tailor the difficulty and types of tasks that lead to earning badges. This ensures that badges are not only challenging but also aligned with each learner's progress and abilities. AI can also automate the tracking and awarding of points and badges, making the system more efficient and scalable. This automation allows for real-time reward issuance and can help keep learners informed of their achievements without delay. Furthermore, AI can analyze comprehensive data to suggest new pathways or additional content that might help learners earn more badges or overcome learning plateaus, thus keeping the training experience dynamic and personalized.

3.1.1.3 Narrative and Storytelling

AI-powered cybersecurity training can significantly benefit from incorporating narrative and storytelling techniques, which serve to enhance the engagement and retention of learning content.[7] Embedding cybersecurity concepts within a compelling narrative enables AI to somewhat transform the training experience into an immersive journey. Thus, making complex information more accessible and memorable. Narratives create a context in which learners can see the practical application of cybersecurity skills in scenarios that mimic real-life challenges, thereby deepening their understanding and emotional investment in the material. Have you ever read a good mystery novel? What if we made that into a cybersecurity mystery novel? That sounds like a fun read.

AI can be instrumental in crafting these stories and integrating them into the cybersecurity curriculum. For example, AI can generate a storyline that evolves based on a learner's decisions and actions within the training modules. This adaptive narrative can create personalized learning experiences where the consequences of a learner's actions directly influence the unfolding of the story. Such dynamic storytelling can significantly increase learner motivation as each participant not only witnesses the impact of their decisions in a simulated world but also feels responsible for the outcomes, whether they be successful resolutions of cybersecurity threats or lessons learned from failures. Furthermore, AI can utilize data from learners' previous interactions to tailor the difficulty and complexity of the tasks within the story, ensuring that each participant is challenged appropriately according to their skill level. This personalized approach helps maintain a steady learning curve and prevents learners from feeling either overwhelmed or under-challenged, which can often detract from engagement.

Narrative-driven training can also facilitate emotional engagement by involving characters that learners can relate to or aspire to emulate.[8] For instance, a narrative could follow a seasoned cybersecurity expert mentoring a novice through various challenges, with learners stepping into the shoes of the novice. As the story progresses, learners tackle increasingly difficult threats, mirroring their real-time skill acquisition in the training. This not only makes the learning process more relatable and engaging but also embeds a deeper understanding of the importance and impact of cybersecurity practices. However, creating such rich, interactive narratives requires careful consideration and design. The narrative must be believable and relevant to the real-world cybersecurity landscape, reflecting actual threats and plausible scenarios. Additionally, the storytelling should not overshadow the educational goals but rather serve to reinforce and elucidate the key concepts being taught. Or in other words, making sure the story does not go off the rails and discuss

---

[7] Shah, Priten. *AI and the Future of Education: Teaching in the Age of Artificial Intelligence*. John Wiley & Sons, 2023.
[8] Jarrah, H., et al. "The impact of storytelling and narrative variables on skill acquisition in gamified learning." *International Journal of Data and Network Science* 8.2 (2024): 1161–1168.

impossible or improbable scenarios (although, a sci-fi cybersecurity training program does sound fun!).

3.1.2 Promoting Active Learning and Skill Acquisition

Section 3.1.2 of this chapter delves into the crucial aspects of promoting active learning and skill acquisition in cybersecurity training, essential components that transform passive listeners into active participants. This section explores various strategies that leverage the dynamic capabilities of AI to foster a more engaged learning environment. We begin by examining how interactive simulations and scenarios can immerse learners in practical, hands-on experiences that mimic real-world cybersecurity challenges. Next, we discuss the importance of immediate feedback and reinforcement, which are vital for correcting mistakes in real-time and solidifying understanding. We then cover the concept of gradual skill progression and mastery, ensuring that learners build confidence as their competencies grow systematically. Lastly, the section highlights the role of collaborative learning and social interaction, which enhance the learning experience by leveraging the diverse perspectives and experiences of peers. Together, these elements form a comprehensive approach to learning that not only equips learners with necessary skills but also ensures they are engaged and motivated throughout their educational journey.

3.1.2.1 Interactive Simulations and Scenarios

One of the most impactful teaching methods involves the use of interactive simulations and scenarios, which are increasingly enhanced by AI-driven gamification. These simulations provide a safe and controlled environment where learners can apply their knowledge and skills to solve problems, respond to threats, and make critical decisions just as they would in real-world situations. This hands-on approach not only reinforces learning but also helps in translating theoretical knowledge into practical skills.

AI-powered simulations are designed to be highly dynamic, adapting to the skill level and progress of each learner to provide a continuously challenging and engaging experience.[9] For example, a beginner might face basic scenarios involving common phishing attacks, while more advanced learners could be tasked with mitigating complex multi-layered security breaches involving coordinated attacks across different systems. This level of customization ensures that learners are neither underwhelmed nor overwhelmed, keeping engagement high and promoting optimal learning outcomes.

---

[9] Dai, Chih-Pu, and Fengfeng Ke. "Educational applications of artificial intelligence in simulation-based learning: A systematic mapping review." *Computers and Education: Artificial Intelligence* 3 (2022): 100087.

Furthermore, these AI-driven scenarios can simulate not just technical challenges but also the pressure and time constraints that come with real cybersecurity incidents. This prepares learners to handle stress and make effective decisions under pressure. AI enhancements allow these scenarios to be richly detailed and highly realistic, often integrating the latest threats and security protocols, thereby ensuring that the training remains up-to-date with current industry standards and practices.

The integration of gamification elements such as scoring, rewards, and competitive elements within these simulations adds an additional layer of motivation.[10] As learners progress through scenarios, they can earn points, badges, or other rewards that acknowledge their mastery and improvement. This not only motivates learners to engage more deeply with the material but also provides a tangible measure of their progress and achievements.

Interactive simulations and scenarios, particularly those enhanced by AI and gamification, present several key benefits in cybersecurity training. These methods significantly enhance learner engagement and retention, as participants are actively involved in applying concepts in real-world-like situations rather than passively receiving information. Such hands-on engagement is crucial for effective learning and memory retention. Moreover, these simulations prepare learners for real-world cybersecurity challenges by allowing them to experience and respond to simulated cyber-attacks in a controlled environment. This not only improves their problem-solving and decision-making skills under pressure but also personalizes the learning experience. AI-driven simulations adapt in complexity based on each learner's performance, providing customized challenges that precisely meet their learning needs. Additionally, these systems offer the advantage of immediate feedback, enabling learners to recognize and correct their mistakes in real time and continuously refine their skills based on AI-generated performance analyses.

However, these advanced training systems come with their own set of challenges. Developing and maintaining AI-enhanced simulations requires substantial investment, as these systems need to incorporate the latest technology and be regularly updated to reflect new cybersecurity threats, resulting in high ongoing costs. There are also accessibility issues to consider; reliance on sophisticated technology can limit the use of such training methods in areas with inadequate technological infrastructure. Furthermore, there is a risk that learners might become overly accustomed to the controlled conditions of simulations, potentially leading to overconfidence that doesn't translate well to the unpredictability of actual cyber threats. Finally, if the training scenarios are not well-aligned with an organization's specific needs and culture, the effectiveness of the training can be compromised. Ensuring that these simulations are tailored to fit the unique challenges and goals of each organization is essential but can be resource-intensive and complex.

---

[10] Nicholson, Scott. "A recipe for meaningful gamification." *Gamification in education and business* (2015): 1–20.
APA

3.1.2.2 Immediate Feedback and Reinforcement

Immediate feedback and reinforcement are pivotal components of AI-powered cybersecurity training, playing a critical role in promoting active learning and facilitating rapid skill acquisition. AI systems excel in providing this kind of feedback efficiently, which is essential for a field as dynamic and critical as cybersecurity. Integrating AI, particularly generative AI, training programs can analyze learner actions in real-time and provide instant feedback. Thus, guiding learners on what they are doing right and what needs improvement.

There are many advantages of using AI for immediate feedback. First, it allows learners to immediately understand the consequences of their actions during training exercises, which reinforces learning by linking actions to outcomes directly.[11] This immediate correlation helps in solidifying knowledge and correcting misconceptions on the spot, which is far more effective than learning about mistakes days or weeks after the fact. Additionally, generative AI can tailor this feedback by generating personalized tips and educational content based on the specific errors a learner makes, thereby enhancing the learning experience with highly relevant and customized advice.

However, implementing such sophisticated AI systems comes with challenges. One significant hurdle is the technical complexity involved in developing AI that can accurately assess complex learner activities and provide meaningful feedback. This requires not only advanced algorithms and processing capabilities but also a deep integration of cybersecurity expertise into the AI's decision-making processes. Furthermore, ensuring that the feedback is delivered in a manner that is constructive and encouraging rather than discouraging or overly critical is crucial, as negative feedback can diminish motivation and hinder learning.

In a practical scenario, an AI-powered cybersecurity training platform could be used within a financial institution to train IT staff on detecting and responding to phishing attacks. As learners engage with simulated phishing scenarios, the AI system would monitor their decisions, such as how they analyze email headers, links, and attachments for signs of phishing. If a learner fails to identify a malicious link, the AI would immediately indicate this mistake, provide a brief explanation of the cues missed, and perhaps even suggest a short, targeted tutorial on spotting such threats. Conversely, when a learner successfully thwarts an attack, the AI would offer positive reinforcement, highlighting what was done correctly. This continuous loop of action, feedback, and additional learning not only keeps the training engaging but also ensures that each learner rapidly acquires and refines the necessary skills. Over time, as the AI collects data on common mistakes and successes, it can also adapt the overall training program, focusing on areas where learners tend to struggle the most, thereby continuously improving the effectiveness of the training offered.

---

[11] Hooda, Monika, et al. "Artificial intelligence for assessment and feedback to enhance student success in higher education." *Mathematical Problems in Engineering* 2022.1 (2022): 5215722.

3.1.2.3 Gradual Skill Progression and Master

Gradual skill progression and mastery are crucial components of effective learning, particularly in complex fields like cybersecurity. Gamification, when enhanced with AI, particularly generative AI, provides a structured pathway for learners to develop and refine their skills systematically over time. This method leverages the capabilities of AI to adapt the difficulty and complexity of challenges based on the learner's evolving competencies, ensuring a continuous and appropriate level of challenge that is essential for sustained learning and skill development. AI supports gradual skill progression by continuously assessing the learner's performance and automatically adjusting the difficulty of tasks. For instance, generative AI can dynamically generate content that addresses specific skill gaps identified during the learning process.[12] As learners master initial concepts, the AI introduces more complex scenarios that require a deeper understanding and more sophisticated responses, thus pushing the learner towards higher levels of mastery. This approach not only maintains engagement by providing an optimal challenge but also ensures that learning is built on a solid foundation of increasingly advanced skills.

However, implementing such AI-driven gamification strategies comes with its set of challenges. The development of AI systems capable of accurately assessing skill levels and generating appropriate content requires significant expertise in both AI programming and cybersecurity. Ensuring the AI's assessments and content adjustments are accurate and beneficial demands ongoing monitoring and refinement, which can be resource-intensive. Additionally, there's the need to balance the progression to keep learners neither too overwhelmed by sudden increases in difficulty nor too unchallenged by a slow pace of advancement.

In a practical setting, an AI-powered cybersecurity training program could be implemented within a corporate environment to enhance the skills of network security teams. Starting with foundational topics like basic network hygiene and threat identification, the AI system would initially present learners with simple tasks such as identifying potential vulnerabilities from a curated list. As learners demonstrate mastery of these concepts, the AI would gradually introduce more complex tasks, such as real-time detection of simulated intrusions or the management of mixed and subtly disguised threats in a controlled virtual environment. Each step would build on the previous one, with the AI analyzing performance and tailoring subsequent tasks to push the boundaries of the learner's capabilities. This scaffolded approach ensures that each team member not only understands theoretical concepts but also acquires practical skills that are critical for their daily responsibilities, thereby enhancing both individual and team proficiency in managing real-world cybersecurity challenges.

---

[12] Jawhar, Shadi, Jeremy Miller, and Zeina Bitar. "AI-Driven Customized Cyber Security Training and Awareness." *2024 IEEE third International Conference on AI in Cybersecurity (ICAIC)*. IEEE, 2024.

3.1.2.4 Collaborative Learning and Social Interaction

Incorporating collaborative learning and social interaction into AI-powered cybersecurity training is a strategic approach to enrich the learning experience, leveraging the social dynamics and collective intelligence of groups.[13] Engaging learners in team challenges or enabling them to share achievements allows training programs to harness the benefits of peer learning and foster a sense of community that enhances educational outcomes.AI, particularly generative AI, can significantly augment these collaborative efforts by facilitating and managing interactions among learners, ensuring they are both meaningful and educationally productive. AI can organize learners into teams based on their skills and learning needs, ensuring a diverse mix of abilities that can enhance team performance and individual learning. During team challenges, AI can monitor interactions and provide real-time suggestions or resources, enhancing the team's ability to solve complex problems together. Furthermore, generative AI can dynamically create group scenarios that require collective decision-making, pushing teams to collaborate under scenarios that mimic real-world cybersecurity crises. Moreover, AI can manage the social sharing of achievements by automating the recognition process. It can publicize learners' accomplishments on leaderboards[14] or within learning networks, providing digital badges or certificates that learners can share across their professional social networks. This not only motivates learners but also promotes an environment of positive reinforcement and community engagement.

Although, before we get too excited, the implementation of collaborative learning and social interaction facilitated by AI comes with challenges. Ensuring that the technology supports meaningful collaboration without replacing human interaction can be complex. There's a delicate balance between using AI to facilitate and enhance collaboration and allowing it to overshadow the human elements that are critical to teamwork and peer learning. Additionally, privacy concerns must be carefully managed, as the system will handle personal performance data and potentially sensitive information about learners' interactions.

Imagine a scenario within a large multinational corporation looking to enhance its cybersecurity defenses through employee training. The organization implements an AI-powered training platform that organizes employees into cross-departmental teams, encouraging a mix of skill levels and backgrounds. Each team is tasked with responding to simulated security threats that require a coordinated approach to identify, analyze, and neutralize threats effectively. The AI system tracks each team's decisions, offering feedback and adjusting scenarios in real-time to keep the challenges appropriate and engaging.

Throughout the training, team achievements are highlighted via an internal platform, where teams can view each other's scores and strategies. This visibility

---

[13] Yuan, Xiaohong, et al. "Teaching cybersecurity using guided inquiry collaborative learning." *2019 IEEE Frontiers in Education Conference (FIE)*. IEEE, 2019.

[14] Khan, Manzoor Ahmed, et al. "Game-based learning platform to enhance cybersecurity education." *Education and Information Technologies* (2022): 1–25.

encourages a healthy competitive spirit and fosters a learning community where teams share insights and strategies. At the end of the training module, teams present their solutions and learnings in a company-wide webinar, facilitated by the AI platform, which consolidates key data points and insights from various team performances to highlight effective strategies and areas for improvement across the company. This approach not only enhances individual and team learning outcomes but also builds a stronger, more collaborative security culture within the organization.

3.2 AI-Powered Immersive Learning Experiences

Section 3.2 delves into the transformative potential of AI-powered immersive learning experiences in cybersecurity training, exploring how advanced technologies can create a more engaging and effective educational environment. This section unpacks the integration of realistic threat scenarios and simulations that leverage AI to provide learners with hands-on, practical experiences that mimic real-world challenges. Additionally, we explore the applications of VR and AR in training, which immerse learners in virtual settings that enhance both the depth and retention of cybersecurity skills. Finally, the chapter discusses the delicate balance between educational value and entertainment—a critical aspect in designing training programs that are not only instructive but also engaging. These elements combine to create a dynamic learning experience that prepares cybersecurity professionals with the skills they need to respond to evolving threats effectively.

3.2.1 Realistic Threat Scenarios and Simulations

AI-powered cybersecurity training excels (and I mean really stands out) in creating realistic threat scenarios and simulations that are both dynamic and adaptive, making use of advanced AI, including generative AI, to tailor experiences to the specific needs of learners. Cybersecurity trainers can especially benefit from realistic scenarios and environments.[15] This advanced technology plays a crucial role in generating scenarios that evolve based on a learner's skill level and progress, ensuring that the challenges remain appropriate to their growing capabilities. Such personalization helps maintain learner engagement and pushes them to continually develop their problem-solving skills without becoming overwhelmed.

Furthermore, AI is instrumental in simulating a wide array of cybersecurity challenges. From basic phishing attacks to complex, multi-layered cyber threats

---

[15] Beuran, Razvan, et al. "Realistic cybersecurity training via scenario progression management." *2019 IEEE European Symposium on Security and Privacy Workshops (EuroS&PW)*. IEEE, 2019.

involving sophisticated malware or ransomware, AI can create diverse scenarios that expose learners to the breadth of potential security threats they might face. This exposure is invaluable for building a well-rounded skill set and preparing learners for anything the real world might throw their way. Moreover, the safe and controlled learning environment provided by AI simulations means that learners can experiment and learn from their mistakes without any real-world repercussions, which is critical for effective learning and experimentation. The complexity of developing AI systems that can accurately simulate advanced cybersecurity threats involves significant investment in terms of time, expertise, and resources. Keeping these simulations up to date with the latest cybersecurity trends and technologies can also be demanding, requiring continuous updates and refinements to the AI algorithms.

A practical implementation of this AI-driven training could be at a financial institution looking to bolster its defense against cyber threats. The institution could deploy an AI-powered training platform where employees engage in monthly cybersecurity drills. These drills would feature a variety of scenarios that reflect the latest real-world threats identified by threat intelligence, adjusted dynamically for different departments based on their specific risk profiles and previous drill performances. For instance, the IT department might face scenarios involving advanced persistent threats while the customer service team could train against social engineering attacks. This tailored training allows employees to develop relevant skills in a realistic yet risk-free setting, ensuring they are prepared to protect the institution's assets effectively.

3.2.1.1 Incorporating Real-World Threat Intelligence

AI-powered cybersecurity training offers a highly dynamic and responsive learning environment that is crucial for preparing professionals to tackle current and emerging cyber threats. Through the integration of advanced AI technologies, cybersecurity training programs can be continuously updated and refined to reflect the rapidly evolving landscape of cyber threats, ensuring that learners are always equipped with the latest knowledge and tools to protect their organizations.

One of the key strengths of AI in cybersecurity training is its ability to integrate real-time data about current and emerging threats into training modules. Emerging and current threat scenarios and simulations are needed for effective cybersecurity training so that learners can be prepared for the current cyber and threat landscape.[16] This involves using algorithms that can analyze vast amounts of threat intelligence from various sources, identifying patterns and trends that are relevant to the training objectives. For example, if a new type of ransomware begins to spread globally, AI systems can quickly incorporate scenarios involving this ransomware into the training curriculum, providing learners with practical experiences in detecting and

---

[16] Urias, Vincent E., et al. "Dynamic cybersecurity training environments for an evolving cyber workforce." *2017 IEEE International Symposium on Technologies for Homeland Security (HST)*. IEEE, 2017.

mitigating this specific threat. Moreover, AI facilitates continuous updates to the training content based on real-world incidents and trends. This capability ensures that the training remains relevant and effective over time. AI systems can automatically revise and enhance training scenarios as new data becomes available, adjusting the complexity and scope of simulations to match the latest security challenges. This continuous learning loop not only keeps the curriculum current but also helps cybersecurity professionals stay ahead of potential attackers by exposing them to the most recent tactics, techniques, and procedures used in the industry.

Additionally, AI-driven training helps in developing and refining the skills necessary to counter evolving cyber risks.[17] Engaging with AI-generated scenarios that simulate real-world attacks allows learners to practice their response strategies in a controlled environment that closely mirrors actual situations they may face. This hands-on approach is invaluable for building practical skills and confidence, which are critical for effectively responding to and mitigating cyber threats. AI's capability to tailor these scenarios based on individual performance further enhances skill development, ensuring that each learner is challenged appropriately according to their existing knowledge and skill level.

In practice, implementing AI-driven cybersecurity training could involve setting up a simulation center where learners engage in monthly security drills that reflect the latest threats. Each session could be tailored to the specific needs of different teams within an organization, with scenarios ranging from data breaches and phishing to advanced persistent threats and insider attacks. As learners progress, the AI system would analyze their responses, provide targeted feedback, and adjust future scenarios to better address any identified weaknesses, thereby ensuring continuous skill development and preparedness for real-world cyber challenges.

Integrating diverse data sources is an important factor to consider here when it comes to AI being able to incorporate real world threat intelligence.[18] The integration of diverse data streams into an AI system for cybersecurity training is a complex task. This process involves collecting, normalizing, and processing data from various sources such as real-time cyber threat feeds, historical incident reports, and emerging trends in cybersecurity threats. For small and medium-sized enterprises (SMEs), the challenges are compounded by limited resources and expertise in handling and analyzing big data. Moreover, ensuring the security and privacy of the data while it is being integrated and processed by AI systems adds another layer of complexity.

To mitigate these challenges, the deployment of lightweight AI systems and AI as a Service (AIaaS) offers a practical solution.[19] Lightweight AI systems are

---

[17] Sarker, Iqbal H. *AI-driven cybersecurity and threat intelligence: cyber automation, intelligent decision-making and explainability*. Springer Nature, 2024

[18] Wagner, Thomas D., et al. "Cyber threat intelligence sharing: Survey and research directions." *Computers & Security* 87 (2019): 101589.

[19] Tsai, Lin, Tang Ying-Chan, and Wang Yu-Mei. "An Empirical Study Of The Competitive Advantage And Strategy In Aiaas Industry." *Commerce & Management Quarterly* 23.4 (2022): 467–504.

designed to require minimal resources, making them ideal for SMEs that might not have the capacity to handle large-scale, resource-intensive AI implementations. These systems can perform essential functions without the overhead associated with more comprehensive systems.

AIaaS, on the other hand, provides AI capabilities as a service, allowing organizations to leverage advanced AI technologies without the need for extensive in-house AI expertise or infrastructure.[20] This model enables SMEs to access state-of-the-art AI tools for cybersecurity training by subscribing to services that manage the AI operations off-site. AIaaS providers can offer tailored solutions that meet the specific needs of the organization, including the integration and analysis of diverse data sources necessary for creating dynamic training content.[21]

To address data privacy concerns and the challenges of managing large volumes of data, decentralization and federated learning are effective strategies. Decentralization involves distributing the data processing tasks across multiple devices or locations, which not only enhances data privacy by minimizing centralized data storage but also reduces the load on any single system, making the AI system more scalable and robust.

Federated learning, a subset of decentralized learning, allows AI models to be trained across multiple decentralized devices or servers holding local data samples, without exchanging them.[22] This method is particularly beneficial for privacy-preserving data analysis, as it enables the AI to learn from a wide variety of data points without actually having access to the raw data. Federated learning can dynamically adjust the algorithms based on the volume and variety of data, optimizing the training modules as new data becomes available while maintaining the confidentiality of the data sources.

Implementing these technologies, while beneficial, is not without its difficulties. The initial setup of federated learning systems and the integration of AIaaS into existing cybersecurity training frameworks can be technically challenging and may require upfront investment in terms of time and finances. However, the long-term benefits—enhanced training effectiveness, scalability, and improved data privacy—often justify the initial efforts. To mitigate implementation challenges, organizations can start with pilot projects to assess the viability and performance of AI systems before full-scale deployment. Partnering with experienced AI service providers can also ease the transition, providing access to expert knowledge and support throughout the process.

---

[20] Musabimana Boneza, Benedicte. "AN INTEGRATION ARCHITECTURE OF AIAAS: INTEROPERABILITY AND FUNCTIONAL SUITABILITY." (2023).

[21] Cobbe, Jennifer, and Jatinder Singh. "Artificial intelligence as a service: Legal responsibilities, liabilities, and policy challenges." *Computer Law & Security Review* 42 (2021): 105573.

[22] Yang, Qiang, et al. "Federated machine learning: Concept and applications." *ACM Transactions on Intelligent Systems and Technology (TIST)* 10.2 (2019): 1–19.

3.2.1.2 Personalized Feedback and Guidance

AI-powered cybersecurity training can leverage advanced analytical capabilities to enhance the learning experience by providing in-depth analysis of learner decisions and actions, targeted recommendations for improvement, and reinforcement of best practices.[23] These aspects are crucial for developing and refining cybersecurity skills effectively.

Utilizing AI, specifically generative AI, cybersecurity training programs can closely monitor and analyze every decision and action taken by learners during simulations and training exercises. This continuous monitoring allows the AI to understand patterns in learner behavior, identify common mistakes, and recognize areas of strength and weakness. Thus, by analyzing those details, AI systems can create highly detailed feedback that helps learners understand what they did right or wrong in a given scenario. Consequently, providing them with concrete examples of how they can improve.

Based on the analysis conducted, AI can generate personalized recommendations for each learner.[24] These recommendations are tailored to address specific gaps or weaknesses identified during the training sessions. For example, if a learner consistently fails to recognize certain types of phishing attacks, the AI can suggest targeted exercises focusing on that particular vulnerability, recommend additional reading materials, or provide mini-lectures (mini or short being the key word here for continued engagement and attention) explaining the nuances of different phishing techniques. This targeted approach ensures that training is not just broad and comprehensive but also deeply personalized to maximize learning efficiency.

AI systems are particularly adept at reinforcing cybersecurity best practices by consistently integrating these into training scenarios and providing reminders and explanations during critical teaching moments. Over time, this method helps ingrain essential habits and reflexes in learners, making best practices second nature. Furthermore, by using generative AI, training modules can evolve based on the latest cybersecurity research and emerging threats, ensuring that learners are always practicing with the most up-to-date information and techniques.

Implementing such sophisticated AI-powered training systems is not without challenges.[25] The complexity of developing an AI that can not only analyze complex human actions but also generate useful feedback and personalized recommendations requires significant expertise in both AI development and cybersecurity. Additionally, these systems need to handle large volumes of sensitive data securely, posing challenges in data privacy and security. Moreover, in terms of ethical

---

[23] Kadaruddin, Kadaruddin. "Empowering education through Generative AI: Innovative instructional strategies for tomorrow's learners." *International Journal of Business, Law, and Education* 4.2 (2023): 618–625.

[24] Tavakoli, Mohammadreza, et al. "An AI-based open recommender system for personalized labor market driven education." *Advanced Engineering Informatics* 52 (2022): 101508.

[25] Fountaine, Tim, Brian McCarthy, and Tamim Saleh. "Building the AI-powered organization." *Harvard Business Review* 97.4 (2019): 62–73.

considerations, it is crucial to understand data privacy legal requirements and best practices. Under the EU AI Act, AI systems that are used in education are considered high risk.[26] Subsequently, privacy is a primary concern and ensuring that data collection and analysis are transparent and consensual is of the utmost importance. Therefore, mitigating these challenges involves a robust design phase where security and privacy are foundational priorities. Employing advanced encryption for data storage and transmission, using secure coding practices, and adhering to compliance standards can help address security concerns. Furthermore, starting with pilot programs can allow organizations to tackle and refine technical and operational issues on a smaller scale before full implementation.

3.2.2 *Virtual Reality and Augmented Reality Applications*

VR and AR are transforming the landscape of cybersecurity training, providing highly immersive environments that can significantly enhance the effectiveness of learning and skill acquisition.[27] AI plays a crucial role in optimizing these VR and AR training environments by enabling realistic, interactive scenarios that mimic real-world cybersecurity settings.

Immersive Cybersecurity Training Environments AI can enrich VR and AR training environments with complex, dynamic simulations. These environments allow learners to engage in realistic scenarios that would be impractical or impossible to replicate in a traditional classroom or online setting. For example, AI can simulate a cyber-attack on a virtual network in real-time, requiring learners to respond and interact with the system just as they would in real life. This level of immersion helps learners understand the implications of their actions in a visceral, hands-on manner, enhancing both learning and retention.

Virtual SOCs (Security Operations Centers) One specific application is the creation of virtual SOCs in VR. Here, learners can experience the high-pressure environment of a real SOC, including monitoring live feeds, responding to threats, and collaborating with team members.[28] AI enhances these simulations by generating live data streams and realistic threat scenarios, providing a robust platform for practical training and decision-making under stress.

---

[26] Edwards, Lilian. "The EU AI Act: a summary of its significance and scope." *Artificial Intelligence (the EU AI Act)* 1 (2021).

[27] Qawasmeh, Saif Al-Dean, Ali Abdullah S. AlQahtani, and Muhammad Khurram Khan. "Navigating Cybersecurity Training: A Comprehensive Review." *arXiv preprint arXiv:2401.11326* (2024).

[28] Diamantopoulos, Dionysios, et al. "Plug&chip: A framework for supporting rapid prototyping of 3d hybrid virtual socs." *ACM Transactions on Embedded Computing Systems (TECS)* 13.5s (2014): 1–25.

Simulated Server Rooms and Office Spaces AI-powered VR can also simulate server rooms and office spaces where physical security measures are just as crucial as cybersecurity protocols.[29] Learners can practice identifying and rectifying security weaknesses, such as unsecured terminals or poorly configured networks, in a controlled virtual setting. This comprehensive approach ensures that learners are prepared to address cybersecurity from multiple angles.

Realistic Settings for Skill Practice and Application The use of AR in cybersecurity training allows for the overlay of digital information onto the real world, offering hands-on practice in actual work environments.[30] For instance, through AR glasses, learners could see cybersecurity warnings and data overlaid on the actual hardware they are using, bridging the gap between theoretical knowledge and practical application.

Through VR and AR, learners can interact with virtual reproductions of complex cybersecurity software and hardware, providing a safe yet realistic setting for mastering the use of these tools. AI enhances these simulations by dynamically adjusting the complexity of the tools and the scenarios based on the user's progress, ensuring that each learner's experience is tailored to their learning curve. This interaction is crucial for understanding the actual functionalities and potential applications of various cybersecurity technologies without the risk of impacting real-world systems.

VR and AR simulations facilitated by AI allow learners to practice and refine technical skills in a controlled environment that mirrors real-world settings. These simulations can include tasks like setting up firewalls, securing network endpoints, or conducting forensic investigations on virtual networks. The immersive nature of VR and AR ensures that learners not only learn about theoretical best practices but also apply them in practice, thereby gaining a deeper understanding and familiarity with the technologies they will use in their professional lives. The ultimate goal of AI-powered VR and AR training is to prepare learners for real-world cybersecurity tasks. Practicing in simulations that closely resemble actual work environments and scenarios, learners can better translate their virtual experiences to real situations. This preparation is critical, especially in cybersecurity, where professionals often need to respond swiftly and effectively to threats to protect organizational assets.

This is important for enhanced situation awareness and decision making. Immersing learners in high-pressure scenarios that require immediate response allows AI-driven simulations to help trainees develop the ability to maintain

---

[29] Jetter, Hans-Christian, et al. ""in vr, everything is possible!": Sketching and simulating spatially-aware interactive spaces in virtual reality." *Proceedings of the 2020 CHI conference on human factors in computing systems*. 2020.

[30] Wagner, Paul, and Dalal Alharthi. "Leveraging VR/AR/MR/XR Technologies to Improve Cybersecurity Education, Training, and Operations." *Journal of Cybersecurity Education, Research and Practice* 2024.1 (2023): 7.

composure and clarity of thought under stress.[31] These scenarios, which can mimic anything from a data breach to a full-scale cyber-attack, are designed to reflect the intensity and pressure of real cybersecurity emergencies. Moreover, AI-enhanced simulations analyze how learners respond to different situations, providing feedback and guidance on improving decision-making processes. This training is invaluable for developing the ability to make quick, informed decisions in high-stakes environments, a critical skill for any cybersecurity professional.

3.2.3 Balancing Educational Value and Entertainment

3.2.3.1 Engaging Storylines and Narratives

Balancing educational value and entertainment in cybersecurity training is crucial for maintaining engagement and enhancing learning outcomes. Integrating engaging storylines and narratives enables training programs to captivate learners' attention and provide a context that makes learning both impactful and memorable. Generative AI, with its ability to create dynamic content, plays a pivotal role in this process by developing compelling narratives that are not only engaging but also deeply educational.

Generative AI can craft storylines that seamlessly integrate educational content within an appealing narrative framework.[32] These narratives can transform mundane training modules into intriguing stories that unfold as the learner progresses. Thus, by incorporating compelling storylines into the educational content, AI helps to create a rich, emotionally resonant context that enhances the absorption and retention of information. For instance, a cybersecurity training program might use a narrative that revolves around a fictional company facing various cyber threats, with learners needing to step in and make decisions that will impact the company's fate.

The power of narrative in training lies in its ability to connect with learners on an emotional level.[33] Generative AI can be programmed to develop scenarios that elicit emotional responses such as tension, empathy, or satisfaction from overcoming challenges. This emotional engagement is particularly effective in cybersecurity training, where understanding the human factors and potential consequences of security breaches is crucial. For example, a scenario might involve a hospital under a ransomware attack, where the learner's actions could directly affect patient care

---

[31] Chowdhury, Noman H., Marc TP Adam, and Geoffrey Skinner. "The impact of time pressure on cybersecurity behaviour: a systematic literature review." *Behaviour & Information Technology* 38.12 (2019): 1290–1308.

[32] Balasubramani, Shipra. *Crafting Narratives: Real-Time Generative Storytelling through Tangible AI.* Diss. OCAD University, 2024.

[33] Antony, Victor Nikhil, and Chien-Ming Huang. "ID. 8: Co-Creating Visual Stories with Generative AI." *ACM Transactions on Interactive Intelligent Systems* (2023).

3.2 AI-Powered Immersive Learning Experiences

and safety. Such scenarios make the implications of cybersecurity vivid and real, encouraging learners to internalize best practices deeply.

Narratives created by AI can also maintain motivation and investment in continuous skill development. Therefore, positioning the learner as a protagonist in a story where their decisions have meaningful consequences, AI-driven narratives make the training process more relevant and engaging. Learners are not just passive recipients of information but active participants in a story that depends on their newly acquired skills to reach a successful resolution. This method ensures that learners see the direct value of their training and are motivated to advance their skills further.

Using generative AI to embed cybersecurity training within a narrative framework allows trainers to put learners in situations that require them to examine the implications of their decisions. This approach is especially potent in demonstrating the fallout from irresponsible, ignorant, or fatigued decision-making. For example, AI can simulate a scenario where a fatigued employee must decide whether to download an email attachment without proper checks, leading to a series of events based on their choice. Such simulations not only highlight the importance of vigilance in cybersecurity but also prepare learners to handle similar stressful situations in real life. Plus, it saves time of a fatigued person having to come up with a realistic narrative for cybersecurity training—generative AI can do it for us!

3.2.3.2 Pacing and Progression Design

In AI-powered cybersecurity training, the design of pacing and progression[34] is crucial in maintaining an optimal balance between educational value and entertainment. This balance ensures that training is not only effective but also engaging, helping learners to remain focused and motivated throughout their learning journey. A well-designed training program introduces new concepts and challenges at a pace that aligns with the learner's ability to absorb and apply new information. AI plays a pivotal role here by analyzing learners' performance data in real-time and adjusting the complexity of the training material accordingly. This adaptive learning approach ensures that concepts are introduced as learners become ready to understand and tackle them, preventing feelings of overwhelm or boredom. Thus, maintaining an appropriate challenge level, AI helps keep the training both stimulating and educational.

Effective pacing must also consider how rewards and progression are structured. In AI-powered training systems, progression through levels or modules can be tied to specific achievements and milestones, with rewards such as badges, points, or unlocking of advanced content used to mark significant accomplishments. This gamification strategy maintains learner engagement by providing continuous motivation and visible markers of progress. AI can optimize this process by ensuring that

---

[34] Abdulhussein, Mustafa. "The Impact of Artificial Intelligence and Machine Learning on Organizations Cybersecurity." (2024).

rewards are given at critical points where they might have the most psychological impact, encouraging learners to continue engaging with the material.

Maintaining learner motivation over the course of their training journey is essential for the successful completion of the program.[35] AI systems can monitor signs of decreasing engagement or performance plateaus and can intervene by introducing varied content formats, interactive elements, or collaborative tasks that reignite interest and participation. Consequently, continually adjusting the training experience to cater to the needs and preferences of learners, AI ensures that motivation remains high from start to finish.

Consider a cybersecurity training program at a large corporation where employees must periodically update their cybersecurity knowledge and skills. An AI-powered training platform could structure the program to begin with a comprehensive assessment to gauge each employee's current level of knowledge. Based on the results, the AI system would tailor the introduction of new concepts, starting with foundational knowledge for some while presenting more advanced challenges to others. As employees progress, the AI system tracks their engagement and performance, adjusting the difficulty of the simulations and introducing new scenarios at an optimal pace to keep the training challenging yet manageable. Rewards (as discussed earlier in this chapter) like digital badges or access to exclusive webinars on cutting-edge topics in cybersecurity could be awarded for completing difficult modules or for continuous participation.

3.2.3.3 Continuous Improvement Through Learning Analytics

Continuous improvement through learning analytics is a critical aspect of AI-powered cybersecurity training, particularly when balancing educational value and entertainment.[36] This approach leverages AI's ability to collect and analyze vast amounts of data to enhance the effectiveness and enjoyment of learning experiences. However, the implementation of such systems comes with several challenges, particularly in the context of new AI regulations.

AI systems in cybersecurity training can continuously monitor how learners interact with the training material, track their performance across different tasks, and collect their feedback on the training experience. This data is crucial for understanding what aspects of the training are working well and which areas need improvement. Subsequently, by tracking these elements, organizations can dynamically adjust the content, difficulty level, and delivery methods to better suit the learner's needs and preferences. Through detailed analytics, AI can identify patterns and trends in learner behavior that may not be immediately apparent. This includes preferences for certain types of content delivery (such as visual versus textual

---

[35] Hatzivasilis, George, et al. "Modern aspects of cyber-security training and continuous adaptation of programmes to trainees." *Applied Sciences* 10.16 (2020): 5702.

[36] Aldoseri, Abdulaziz, Khalifa N. Al-Khalifa, and Abdel Magid Hamouda. "AI-Powered Innovation in Digital Transformation: Key Pillars and Industry Impact." *Sustainability* 16.5 (2024): 1790.

3.2 AI-Powered Immersive Learning Experiences

information) or common struggles with specific cybersecurity concepts. Analyzing this data allows AI to help tailor the learning experience to maximize both educational outcomes and learner satisfaction.

The data collected and analyzed by AI allows for the refinement of training modules to optimize learning outcomes and enhance the enjoyment factor of the training.[37] This might involve adjusting the gamification elements to make them more engaging or redesigning scenarios to be more reflective of real-world applications, thereby making the learning experience both more enjoyable and practically valuable.

Implementing continuous improvement through learning analytics is not without challenges, particularly regarding compliance with new regulations such as the EU AI Act,[38] the Colorado AI Act,[39] and relevant state laws (like in California[40]) and GDPR[41] provisions. These laws classify educational AI systems as high-risk, mandating strict compliance to ensure that the systems are safe, transparent, and do not violate privacy rights. Organizations must design their AI-powered training systems to adhere to these laws, which often requires developing a comprehensive compliance program. This program must address aspects like data protection, where GDPR requires that personal data be handled in ways that ensure privacy and confidentiality. Similarly, the AI Act and similar regulations may require that systems are transparent in their operations and decision-making processes, particularly when these decisions directly affect the learners' educational or professional opportunities.

To maintain compliance, organizations will need to invest in legal and technical expertise to ensure that their AI systems do not inadvertently breach these regulations. This includes conducting regular audits of the AI's algorithms and data handling practices, maintaining a clear chain of custody for all data used, and ensuring that all data processing activities are lawful, fair, and transparent. Additionally, it is essential to have mechanisms in place to handle any data breaches or non-compliance issues swiftly and effectively.

---

[37] Chen, Zhisheng. "Artificial intelligence-virtual trainer: Innovative didactics aimed at personalized training needs." *Journal of the Knowledge Economy* 14.2 (2023): 2007–2025.

[38] Veale, Michael, and Frederik Zuiderveen Borgesius. "Demystifying the Draft EU Artificial Intelligence Act—Analysing the good, the bad, and the unclear elements of the proposed approach." *Computer Law Review International* 22.4 (2021): 97–112.

[39] The Colorado AI Act. IAPP. https://iapp.org/news/a/the-colorado-ai-act-what-you-need-to-know

[40] SB-1288 Public Schools: Artificial Intelligence Working Group. California Legislative Information. https://leginfo.legislature.ca.gov/faces/billStatusClient.xhtml?bill_id=202320240SB1288

[41] Sartor, Giovanni, and Francesca Lagioia. "The impact of the General Data Protection Regulation (GDPR) on artificial intelligence." (2020): 1–84.

References

1. Sharma, R., & Thapa, S. (2023). Cybersecurity awareness, education, and behavioral change: Strategies for promoting secure online practices among end users. *Eigenpub Review of Science and Technology, 7*(1), 224–238.
2. Kam, H.-J., et al. (2020). Cultivating cybersecurity learning: An integration of self-determination and flow. *Computers & Security, 96*, 101875.
3. Lee, D., Lallie, H. S., & Michaelides, N. (2023). The impact of an employee's psychological contract breach on compliance with information security policies: Intrinsic and extrinsic motivation. *Cognition, Technology & Work, 25*(2), 273–289.
4. Malone, M., et al. (2021). To gamify or not? on leaderboard effects, student engagement and learning outcomes in a cybersecurity intervention. In *Proceedings of the 52nd ACM Technical Symposium on Computer Science Education*.
5. Balon, T., & Baggili, I. (2023). Cybercompetitions: A survey of competitions, tools, and systems to support cybersecurity education. *Education and Information Technologies, 28*(9), 11759–11791.
6. Mclaughlin, K. (2023). *A quantitative study of learner choice in cybersecurity training: Do they even want gamification?* Diss. Colorado Technical University.
7. Shah, P. (2023). *AI and the future of education: Teaching in the age of artificial intelligence*. Wiley.
8. Jarrah, H., et al. (2024). The impact of storytelling and narrative variables on skill acquisition in gamified learning. *International Journal of Data and Network Science, 8*(2), 1161–1168.
9. Dai, C.-P., & Ke, F. (2022). Educational applications of artificial intelligence in simulation-based learning: A systematic mapping review. *Computers and Education: Artificial Intelligence, 3*, 100087.
10. Nicholson, S. (2015). A recipe for meaningful gamification. *Gamification in Education and Business*, 1–20.
11. Hooda, M., et al. (2022). Artificial intelligence for assessment and feedback to enhance student success in higher education. *Mathematical Problems in Engineering, 2022*(1), 5215722.
12. Jawhar, S., Miller, J., & Bitar, Z. (2024). AI-driven customized cyber security training and awareness. In *2024 IEEE 3rd international conference on AI in cybersecurity (ICAIC)*. IEEE.
13. Yuan, X., et al. (2019). Teaching cybersecurity using guided inquiry collaborative learning. In *2019 IEEE Frontiers in Education Conference (FIE)*. IEEE.
14. Khan, M. A., et al. (2022). Game-based learning platform to enhance cybersecurity education. *Education and Information Technologies*, 1–25.
15. Beuran, R., et al. (2019). Realistic cybersecurity training via scenario progression management. In *2019 IEEE European symposium on security and privacy workshops (EuroS&PW)*. IEEE.
16. Urias, V. E., et al. (2017). Dynamic cybersecurity training environments for an evolving cyber workforce. In *2017 IEEE international symposium on Technologies for Homeland Security (HST)*. IEEE.
17. Sarker, I. H. (2024). *AI-driven cybersecurity and threat intelligence: Cyber automation, intelligent decision-making and explainability*. Springer Nature.
18. Wagner, T. D., et al. (2019). Cyber threat intelligence sharing: Survey and research directions. *Computers & Security, 87*, 101589.
19. Tsai, L., Ying-Chan, T., & Yu-Mei, W. (2022). An empirical study of the competitive advantage and strategy in AIAAS industry. *Commerce & Management Quarterly, 23*(4), 467–504.
20. Musabimana Boneza, B. (2023). *An integration architecture of AIAAS: Interoperability and functional suitability*.
21. Cobbe, J., & Singh, J. (2021). Artificial intelligence as a service: Legal responsibilities, liabilities, and policy challenges. *Computer Law & Security Review, 42*, 105573.
22. Yang, Q., et al. (2019). Federated machine learning: Concept and applications. *ACM Transactions on Intelligent Systems and Technology (TIST), 10*(2), 1–19.

References

23. Kadaruddin, K. (2023). Empowering education through generative AI: Innovative instructional strategies for tomorrow's learners. *International Journal of Business, Law, and Education, 4*(2), 618–625.
24. Tavakoli, M., et al. (2022). An AI-based open recommender system for personalized labor market driven education. *Advanced Engineering Informatics, 52*, 101508.
25. Fountaine, T., McCarthy, B., & Saleh, T. (2019). Building the AI-powered organization. *Harvard Business Review, 97*(4), 62–73.
26. Edwards, L. (2021). The EU AI act: A summary of its significance and scope. *Artificial Intelligence (the EU AI Act), 1*.
27. Qawasmeh, S. A.-D., AlQahtani, A. A. S., & Khan, M. K. (2024). Navigating cybersecurity training: A comprehensive review. *arXiv preprint arXiv, 2401*, 11326.
28. Diamantopoulos, D., et al. (2014). Plug&chip: A framework for supporting rapid prototyping of 3d hybrid virtual socs. *ACM Transactions on Embedded Computing Systems (TECS), 13*(5s), 1–25.
29. Jetter, H.-C., et al. (2020). "in VR, everything is possible!": Sketching and simulating spatially-aware interactive spaces in virtual reality. *Proceedings of the 2020 CHI conference on human factors in computing systems*.
30. Wagner, P., & Alharthi, D. (2023). Leveraging VR/AR/MR/XR technologies to improve cybersecurity education, training, and operations. *Journal of Cybersecurity Education, Research and Practice, 2024*(1), 7.
31. Chowdhury, N. H., Adam, M. T. P., & Skinner, G. (2019). The impact of time pressure on cybersecurity behaviour: A systematic literature review. *Behaviour & Information Technology, 38*(12), 1290–1308.
32. Balasubramani, S. (2024). *Crafting narratives: Real-time generative storytelling through tangible AI*. Diss. OCAD University.
33. Antony, V. N., & Huang, C.-M. (2023). ID. 8: Co-creating visual stories with generative AI. *ACM Transactions on Interactive Intelligent Systems*.
34. Abdulhussein, M. (2024). The impact of artificial intelligence and machine learning on organizations cybersecurity.
35. Hatzivasilis, G., et al. (2020). Modern aspects of cyber-security training and continuous adaptation of programmes to trainees. *Applied Sciences, 10*(16), 5702.
36. Aldoseri, A., Al-Khalifa, K. N., & Hamouda, A. M. (2024). AI-powered innovation in digital transformation: Key pillars and industry impact. *Sustainability, 16*(5), 1790.
37. Chen, Z. (2023). Artificial intelligence-virtual trainer: Innovative didactics aimed at personalized training needs. *Journal of the Knowledge Economy, 14*(2), 2007–2025.
38. Veale, M., & Borgesius, F. Z. (2021). Demystifying the draft EU artificial intelligence act—Analysing the good, the bad, and the unclear elements of the proposed approach. *Computer Law Review International, 22*(4), 97–112.
39. TheColoradoAIAct.IAPP.https://iapp.org/news/a/the-colorado-ai-act-what-you-need-to-know
40. SB-1288 Public Schools: Artificial Intelligence Working Group. California Legislative Information. https://leginfo.legislature.ca.gov/faces/billStatusClient.xhtml?bill_id=202320240SB1288
41. Sartor, G., & Lagioia, F. (2020). *The impact of the General Data Protection Regulation (GDPR) on artificial intelligence* (pp. 1–84).

Chapter 4
AI-Generated Realistic Threat Scenarios

This chapter delves into the transformative role of artificial intelligence in cybersecurity education, focusing on its capacity to generate dynamic and evolving threat simulations. This chapter explores how AI can bridge the gap between theoretical knowledge and practical application, preparing learners for the complexities of real-world cybersecurity challenges. By examining the importance of realistic threat scenarios, the mechanics of AI-driven scenario generation, and the enhancement of training content through AI-generated elements, we uncover the potential for more effective, engaging, and adaptable cybersecurity training. The chapter also addresses the critical aspects of measuring scenario effectiveness and the ethical considerations surrounding AI-generated threat simulations, ensuring a comprehensive approach to this cutting-edge educational methodology.

4.1 The Importance of Realistic Threat Scenarios in Training

The cornerstone of effective cybersecurity education lies in the use of realistic threat scenarios. This section explores how exposing learners to authentic cybersecurity situations bridges the gap between theory and practice, enhances situational awareness, and builds confidence in handling real threats. This chapter also examines how these scenarios develop crucial practical skills and decision-making abilities, focusing on honing critical thinking under pressure, improving response time and accuracy, and fostering adaptive problem-solving skills. Immersing learners in lifelike challenges, this chapter demonstrates how to prepare them to face the dynamic and unpredictable nature of real-world cybersecurity threats with competence and agility.

© The Author(s), under exclusive license to Springer Nature Switzerland AG 2025
S. Rana, R. Chicone, *Fortifying the Future*,
https://doi.org/10.1007/978-3-031-81780-9_4

4.1.1 Exposing Learners to Authentic Cybersecurity Situations

Exposing learners to authentic cybersecurity situations is crucial in cybersecurity training, as it provides a practical context for theoretical knowledge and prepares professionals for real-world challenges.[1] AI-powered cyber training, particularly leveraging generative AI, has revolutionized this aspect of education by creating highly realistic and dynamic scenarios that closely mimic actual cyber threats. These AI-generated situations can adapt in real-time to learners' actions, providing a more immersive and responsive training environment than traditional static methods. We often hear about how there are so many cybersecurity jobs that are unfilled because of the lack of experience and human capital. Consequently, revolutionizing cybersecurity training could be a turning point when it comes to having qualified individuals to fill these cybersecurity jobs.

Generative AI's capability to create diverse and evolving scenarios is particularly game-changing. It can produce an almost limitless variety of authentic-feeling cybersecurity situations, from sophisticated phishing attempts to complex multi-vector attacks, ensuring that learners are exposed to a wide range of potential threats. This diversity helps build a more comprehensive skill set and prepares professionals for the unpredictable nature of real-world cyber attacks. Moreover, AI can tailor these scenarios to specific industries or roles, making the training more relevant and applicable to each learner's particular context.[2] As discussed earlier, this requires significant investment in technology and expertise to develop and maintain sophisticated AI systems. There's also the need to ensure that the AI-generated scenarios remain accurate and up-to-date with the latest threat landscapes, which demands continuous refinement and updating of the AI models. Additionally, organizations must navigate the ethical considerations and potential biases in AI-generated content, ensuring that the training scenarios are fair, unbiased, and do not inadvertently reinforce stereotypes or misconceptions.

Despite these challenges, the benefits of AI-powered authentic cybersecurity situations in training are substantial. They contribute significantly to building a cybersecurity-aware culture within organizations. Thus, by providing realistic, engaging, and relevant training experiences, AI helps to make cybersecurity more tangible and immediately applicable for all employees, not just IT specialists. This broad-based, experiential learning approach can lead to a more security-conscious workforce, where individuals are better equipped to recognize and respond to potential threats in their day-to-day activities.

In practice, AI-powered cybersecurity training can effectively bridge the gap between theory and practice. For instance, a financial institution could use an AI

---

[1] Shivapurkar, Mandar, Sajal Bhatia, and Irfan Ahmed. "Problem-based learning for cybersecurity education." *Journal of The Colloquium for Information Systems Security Education*. Vol. 7. No. 1. 2020.

[2] Chen, Lijia, Pingping Chen, and Zhijian Lin. "Artificial intelligence in education: A review." *IEEE Access* 8 (2020): 75264–75278.

system to simulate a sophisticated ransomware attack on their network. The AI would generate realistic attack patterns, mimicking the behavior of actual malware, and respond dynamically to the actions taken by the trainees. This could include simulating the encryption of files, generating fake ransom demands, and adapting the attack vector based on the defensive measures employed. Trainees would need to apply their theoretical knowledge in real-time, making decisions on how to contain the threat, communicate with stakeholders, and recover systems. The AI could then provide immediate feedback, highlighting successful strategies and areas for improvement. This hands-on experience allows learners to see the direct application of their knowledge, reinforcing theoretical concepts and building practical skills simultaneously.

4.1.2 Developing Practical Skills and Decision-Making Abilities

AI-powered cybersecurity training offers significant advantages in developing practical skills and decision-making abilities, particularly in honing critical thinking under high-pressure situations. Unlike traditional training methods that often rely on static scenarios or theoretical discussions, AI can generate dynamic, evolving situations that require trainees to think on their feet and make rapid decisions. For instance, an AI system could simulate a multi-vector attack on an organization's network, continuously adapting the threat based on the trainee's responses. This real-time interaction forces learners to critically analyze the situation, prioritize threats, and make quick decisions—skills that are crucial in actual cybersecurity incidents.

In terms of improving response time and accuracy, AI-powered training excels by providing immediate feedback and personalized challenges. The AI can track a trainee's response times to various threats and adjust the pace of scenarios accordingly, gradually increasing speed and complexity to improve reaction times. Moreover, by analyzing patterns in a trainee's decisions, the AI can identify areas where accuracy is lacking and generate targeted scenarios to address these weaknesses. This level of personalization is difficult to achieve with traditional training methods and can lead to more efficient and effective skill development.

AI-powered training is particularly adept at fostering adaptive problem-solving skills.[3] In the rapidly evolving field of cybersecurity, the ability to adapt to new and unforeseen threats is crucial. AI can generate novel scenarios that combine elements of known threats in unexpected ways, challenging trainees to apply their knowledge creatively. This approach helps develop a flexible mindset, encouraging

---

[3] Kallonas, Christos, Andriani Piki, and Eliana Stavrou. "Empowering professionals: a generative AI approach to personalized cybersecurity learning." *2024 IEEE Global Engineering Education Conference (EDUCON)*. IEEE, 2024.

cybersecurity professionals to think outside the box and adapt their strategies to unfamiliar situations. Traditional training often struggles to keep pace with the latest threats, while AI can continuously update its scenarios based on the most recent threat intelligence.[4]

To illustrate the difference between traditional and AI-powered training, consider a scenario where a large financial institution is facing a sophisticated ransomware attack coupled with a distributed denial-of-service (DDoS) attack. In traditional training, this scenario might be presented as a case study or a scripted simulation with predetermined outcomes. Trainees would discuss potential responses or follow a set protocol, but the dynamic nature of a real attack would be hard to replicate.

In contrast, an AI-powered training system could simulate this complex attack in real-time. As the trainee works to mitigate the ransomware threat, the AI could escalate the DDoS attack, simulating increased network traffic and system failures. The AI could then introduce additional complications, such as a potential data breach or a phishing campaign targeting employees during the chaos. This dynamic scenario requires trainees to continuously reassess the situation, prioritize threats, and make quick decisions under pressure. The AI system can provide immediate feedback on each decision, allowing trainees to see the consequences of their actions and learn from mistakes in a safe environment. This level of complexity and immediacy in training scenarios better prepares cybersecurity professionals for the unpredictable and high-stakes nature of real-world cyber attacks. It helps develop professionals who are not just knowledgeable about theoretical concepts, but are also experienced in applying that knowledge under pressure. This approach cultivates a workforce that is more adaptable, quick-thinking, and prepared to face the complex and ever-evolving landscape of cyber threats. As a result, organizations can build more resilient cybersecurity teams capable of responding effectively to a wide range of potential incidents, ultimately enhancing their overall security posture.

4.2 AI-Driven Threat Scenario Generation

This section explores the cutting-edge applications of AI in cybersecurity training, focusing on AI-driven threat scenario generation. It examines how AI analyzes emerging threats and attack patterns, leveraging machine learning for threat intelligence, incorporating real-time cyber threat data, and predicting future attack vectors. This section then delves into the creation of dynamic and adaptive training content, discussing methods for generating varied and evolving threat scenarios, personalizing learning experiences, and scaling difficulty to match skill development. Finally, it covers the integration of hypothetical situations, including simulations of Advanced Persistent Threats (APTs), replications of social engineering

---

[4] Bécue, Adrien, Isabel Praça, and João Gama. "Artificial intelligence, cyber-threats and Industry 4.0: Challenges and opportunities." *Artificial Intelligence Review* 54.5 (2021): 3849–3886.

4.2 AI-Driven Threat Scenario Generation

attacks, and models of insider threat scenarios. Through these topics, the chapter illustrates how AI can create highly realistic and relevant training environments that prepare cybersecurity professionals for the ever-evolving threat landscape.

4.2.1 Analyzing Emerging Threats and Attack Patterns

AI, particularly machine learning algorithms, has revolutionized the analysis of emerging threats and attack patterns in cybersecurity. Leveraging machine learning for threat intelligence, AI systems can process and analyze vast amounts of data from diverse sources, identifying subtle patterns and correlations that might escape human analysts.[5] This capability allows for a more comprehensive and nuanced understanding of the threat landscape, enabling cybersecurity professionals to stay ahead of potential attackers.

Incorporating real-time cyber threat data is another area where AI excels. AI systems can continuously ingest and analyze data from multiple sources, including threat feeds, security logs, and global incident reports.[6] This real-time analysis allows for the immediate detection of new threats and attack methodologies as they emerge. For instance, in the healthcare industry, which is currently facing unprecedented levels of ransomware attacks, AI can quickly identify new ransomware variants or novel attack vectors, allowing for rapid response and mitigation strategies. This real-time capability is far superior to traditional training methods, which often rely on historical data and can quickly become outdated in the fast-paced world of cyber threats.

Perhaps one of the most powerful applications of AI in this context is its ability to predict future attack vectors. AI can forecast potential future threats by analyzing historical data, current trends, and even seemingly unrelated global events. This predictive capability allows organizations to proactively strengthen their defenses against anticipated attacks, rather than merely reacting to known threats. In a post-quantum world, where the landscape of cryptography and cybersecurity is set to dramatically change, this predictive ability will be crucial in preparing for and mitigating new types of quantum-enabled cyber threats.[7]

While the benefits of AI in analyzing emerging threats are clear, implementing such systems does present challenges. Compiling diverse data streams from various sources can be complex, requiring sophisticated data integration and normalization techniques. However, once these challenges are overcome, the resulting

---

[5] Loaiza, Francisco L., et al. *Utility of artificial intelligence and machine learning in cybersecurity.* Institute for Defense Analyses., 2019.

[6] Montasari, Reza, et al. "Application of artificial intelligence and machine learning in producing actionable cyber threat intelligence." *Digital forensic investigation of internet of things (IoT) devices* (2021): 47–64.

[7] Khodaiemehr, Hassan, Khadijeh Bagheri, and Chen Feng. "Navigating the quantum computing threat landscape for blockchains: A comprehensive survey." *Authorea Preprints* (2023).

comprehensive threat intelligence can greatly enhance cyber training. AI is uniquely suited to handle this complexity, capable of processing and making sense of disparate data sources in ways that would be impractical or impossible for human analysts alone.

It's crucial to note that systems accumulating this sensitive threat data must be secured with extreme precautions. The data itself is valuable and could be a target for attackers. However, when properly secured and utilized, this data can provide highly targeted and personalized training. AI can analyze an organization's specific threat profile based on its size, culture, sector, and industry, and tailor training scenarios to address the most relevant and likely threats. This level of customization is far beyond what traditional training methods can offer, resulting in more effective and efficient cybersecurity preparation. As we move towards a post-quantum era, this ability to rapidly adapt training to emerging threats will be invaluable in maintaining robust cybersecurity defenses against increasingly sophisticated and technologically advanced attacks.

When it comes to national security, AI-powered cybersecurity training could bolster national defenses. The application of AI-powered threat analysis and training is particularly crucial for critical infrastructure sectors such as energy, water, transportation, and healthcare.[8] These sectors are prime targets for cyber attacks due to their essential nature and the potentially catastrophic consequences of successful breaches. AI's ability to analyze emerging threats and attack patterns in real-time is invaluable for these high-stakes environments, where even a minor security lapse could have far-reaching impacts on public safety and national security.

For critical infrastructure, AI can provide tailored threat intelligence that takes into account the unique vulnerabilities and potential attack vectors specific to each sector. For instance, in the energy sector, AI could analyze patterns related to industrial control systems (ICS) and SCADA networks, identifying potential threats that could disrupt power grids.[9] In healthcare, AI could focus on threats targeting medical devices and patient data systems.[10] This sector-specific approach allows for more targeted and effective cybersecurity measures. Moreover, AI's predictive capabilities are especially valuable in critical infrastructure protection, as they enable proactive defense strategies against potential future attacks, helping to maintain the continuous operation of essential services. The ability of AI to rapidly process and analyze vast amounts of data from various sources also enhances the overall resilience of critical infrastructure, enabling quicker response times to

---

[8] Sarker, Iqbal H. "AI for Critical Infrastructure Protection and Resilience." *AI-Driven Cybersecurity and Threat Intelligence: Cyber Automation, Intelligent Decision-Making and Explainability* (2024): 153–172.

[9] Singh, Suby, et al. "Artificial intelligence and security of industrial control systems." *Handbook of Big Data Privacy* (2020): 121–164.

[10] Yeng, Prosper Kandabongee, et al. "Data-driven and artificial intelligence (AI) approach for modelling and analyzing healthcare security practice: a systematic review." *Intelligent Systems and Applications:*

4.2.2 Creating Dynamic and Adaptive Training Content

As aforementioned, AI-powered security systems, particularly those leveraging generative AI, are revolutionizing cybersecurity training by creating dynamic and adaptive content that evolves with learners' progress and the changing threat landscape. This approach allows for the generation of varied and evolving threat scenarios that closely mimic real-world situations. Unlike traditional static training modules, AI can produce an almost infinite variety of scenarios, ensuring that learners are constantly exposed to new and challenging situations. This variety is crucial in preparing cybersecurity professionals for the unpredictable nature of actual cyber threats.

We have discussed this extensively; however, it is important to reiterate in the context of threat scenario generation. Personalization of scenarios based on learner progress is another significant advantage of AI-powered training.[11] Analyzing a learner's performance, decision-making patterns, and areas of weakness, AI can tailor scenarios to address specific learning needs. For instance, if a learner consistently struggles with identifying social engineering attacks, the AI can generate more scenarios focused on this area, gradually increasing in complexity as the learner improves. This level of personalization ensures that each learner receives a uniquely optimized training experience, something that is virtually impossible to achieve with traditional training methods. Scaling difficulty to match skill development is a key feature of AI-generated scenarios. As learners progress and demonstrate mastery of certain concepts, the AI can automatically increase the complexity and sophistication of the scenarios presented. This could involve introducing multi-vector attacks, more subtle indicators of compromise, or scenarios that require integration of multiple cybersecurity disciplines. This dynamic scaling ensures that learners are always challenged at the appropriate level, maintaining engagement and promoting continuous skill development.

For a practical example, let's consider a small organization like a local credit union. We have previously examined larger organizations, but SMEs can benefit from AI-powered cybersecurity training. They could implement an AI-powered training system that starts by assessing each employee's current cybersecurity knowledge. Based on this assessment, the AI generates personalized phishing simulation scenarios. For a novice, it might create simple phishing emails with obvious red flags. As the employee successfully identifies these, the AI progressively introduces more sophisticated phishing attempts, perhaps incorporating elements of

---

[11] *Proceedings of the 2020 Intelligent Systems Conference (IntelliSys) Volume 1*. Springer International Publishing, 2021.

spear phishing or whaling attacks tailored to the credit union's specific context. The system continuously adjusts the difficulty based on the employee's performance, ensuring ongoing challenge and learning.

In contrast, a larger organization like a multinational corporation could utilize a more comprehensive AI-powered system. This system could simulate complex, multi-stage attacks across various departments. For instance, it might generate a scenario that begins with a phishing attack on the HR department, escalates to a ransomware infection in the finance department, and culminates in a data exfiltration attempt from the R&D division. The AI would personalize this scenario for different roles within the organization, presenting relevant challenges to each department while maintaining an overarching narrative. As employees from various departments collaborate to address the simulated threat, the AI adjusts the scenario in real-time, introducing new complications or changing attack vectors based on the collective response of the team.

Traditional cybersecurity training simply cannot match this level of dynamism and personalization. Static courses or pre-programmed simulations quickly become outdated and fail to adapt to individual learning needs or emerging threats. Moreover, the resources and human capital required to manually create and update such varied, evolving, and personalized scenarios are prohibitive for most organizations. AI bridges this gap, providing sophisticated, up-to-date training content at scale. The development of these AI-powered training systems relies on advanced machine learning techniques. Generative Adversarial Networks (GANs) can be used to create realistic and diverse threat scenarios by pitting a generator against a discriminator, continuously improving the quality and authenticity of generated content.[12] Variational Autoencoders (VAEs) can help in generating varied scenarios while maintaining certain desired characteristics.[13] Transformative models, particularly large language models, can be employed to generate realistic textual content for phishing emails or social engineering scripts.[14] Neural networks, especially recurrent and convolutional neural networks, play a crucial role in analyzing learner behavior and adapting scenario difficulty.[15] In terms of practical implementation, it's important to understand current training needs and cybersecurity priorities. From there, investing in AI-powered training platforms that offer scenario generation capabilities would be key. Another important consideration is ensuring the

---

[12] Dash, Ankan, Junyi Ye, and Guiling Wang. "A review of generative adversarial networks (GANs) and its applications in a wide variety of disciplines: from medical to remote sensing." *IEEE Access* (2023).

[13] Ivanovic, Boris, et al. "Multimodal deep generative models for trajectory prediction: A conditional variational autoencoder approach." *IEEE Robotics and Automation Letters* 6.2 (2020): 295–302.

[14] Hassanin, Mohammed, and Nour Moustafa. "A Comprehensive Overview of Large Language Models (LLMs) for Cyber Defences: Opportunities and Directions." *arXiv preprint arXiv:2405.14487* (2024).

[15] Li, Zewen, et al. "A survey of convolutional neural networks: analysis, applications, and prospects." *IEEE transactions on neural networks and learning systems* 33.12 (2021): 6999–7019.

chosen system can integrate with existing security tools to incorporate real threat intelligence. A pilot program would be crucial to test the AI system's efficacy and gather feedback.

4.2.3 Example

Imagine an AI-powered training system designed to simulate an APT attack on a fictional multinational corporation. The scenario begins with a seemingly innocuous phishing email sent to an employee in the marketing department. As the trainee investigates, the AI dynamically adjusts the scenario based on their actions.

If the trainee successfully identifies and blocks the initial phishing attempt, the AI might escalate the scenario by simulating a more sophisticated spear-phishing attack targeting a C-level executive. Throughout the simulation, the AI generates realistic network traffic, log entries, and system behaviors that mimic the stealthy nature of APTs.

The trainee must piece together disparate clues, such as unusual data transfers, subtle changes in user behavior, and encrypted communications with unknown servers. The AI continuously adapts the scenario, perhaps introducing new attack vectors or changing tactics if the trainee successfully blocks certain pathways.

This type of dynamic, evolving APT simulation offers several advantages over traditional training:

- It provides a more realistic experience of the persistence and adaptability of real APTs.
- It tests the trainee's ability to correlate information from multiple sources over an extended period.
- It can be personalized based on the trainee's role, skill level, and previous performance.

For social engineering training, an AI system could create a multi-channel attack scenario that evolves based on the trainee's responses. The simulation might start with a series of carefully crafted emails purportedly from IT support, requesting password resets due to a system upgrade If the trainee falls for this initial attempt, the AI could escalate the scenario by simulating follow-up phone calls or instant messages, applying pressure tactics or appealing to authority. If the trainee successfully rebuffs these attempts, the AI might switch tactics, perhaps simulating a physical security breach attempt through tailgating or impersonation.

The AI could generate realistic dialogue for phone conversations, create convincing fake websites for phishing attempts, and even simulate social media profiles for more elaborate social engineering scenarios. This level of detail and adaptability allows for:

- Training that covers a wide range of social engineering tactics and channels.

- Realistic practice in identifying and responding to evolving social engineering attempts.
- Personalized scenarios that target specific vulnerabilities or behaviors observed in the trainee's responses.

Insider threats are particularly challenging to simulate due to their complex nature involving human behavior and organizational context. An AI-powered system could create nuanced scenarios that test a trainee's ability to identify subtle indicators of insider threats.

For example, the AI might generate a scenario where an employee's behavior gradually changes over time. This could include unusual access patterns to sensitive data, changes in working hours, or anomalies in email communications. The trainee would need to monitor various data points and decide when and how to escalate their concerns.

The AI could introduce complications such as:

- False positives: Simulating behavior that seems suspicious but has a legitimate explanation.
- Ethical dilemmas: Creating situations where the suspected insider is a high-performing employee or someone facing personal difficulties.
- Complex motivations: Simulating scenarios where the insider's actions are driven by a mix of factors like financial pressure, disgruntlement, and external coercion.

This type of training offers several benefits:

- It helps develop nuanced judgment in dealing with potential insider threats.
- It can simulate long-term patterns of behavior that would be difficult to replicate in traditional training.
- It allows for the exploration of various response strategies and their consequences.

In all these examples, the use of AI allows for a level of complexity, adaptability, and personalization that traditional training methods cannot match. The AI can generate vast amounts of realistic data, adapt scenarios in real-time based on trainee actions, and provide immediate feedback. This results in more engaging, challenging, and effective cybersecurity training that better prepares professionals for the complexities of real-world threats.

4.3 Enhancing Realism Through AI-Generated Elements

This section delves into the sophisticated ways AI enhances the realism of cybersecurity training scenarios through the generation of lifelike elements. It explores the creation of believable digital artifacts, including realistic phishing emails, simulated malware behaviors and signatures, and convincing network traffic patterns. The

4.3 Enhancing Realism Through AI-Generated Elements

section also examines how AI simulates human behavior in threat scenarios, covering the modeling of user interactions and responses, replication of attacker tactics and techniques, and simulation of organizational dynamics and policies. In general, this section demonstrates how cybersecurity training can achieve unprecedented levels of authenticity, better preparing professionals for the complexities and nuances of real-world cyber threats.

4.3.1 Creating Believable Digital Artifacts

AI, particularly generative AI, has revolutionized the creation of believable digital artifacts for cybersecurity training.[16] This capability is crucial in developing realistic and effective training scenarios that closely mimic real-world cyber threats. When it comes to generating realistic phishing emails, AI can analyze vast datasets of genuine and malicious emails to understand the nuances of language, formatting, and social engineering tactics used by attackers. This can be done by feeding the AI system with examples of both legitimate corporate communications and known phishing attempts. Subsequently, it can generate highly convincing phishing emails that reflect current trends and tactics. These AI-generated emails can incorporate elements like company logos, signature styles, and contextual information that make them particularly challenging to distinguish from genuine communications.

Simulating malware behavior and signatures is another area where AI excels. Thus, training AI models on a wide range of malware samples, including their behavior patterns, code structures, and signature characteristics, the system can generate simulated malware that exhibits realistic traits. This capability allows for the creation of safe, yet highly authentic training environments where cybersecurity professionals can practice detecting and analyzing malware without the risks associated with real malicious software. The AI can simulate various types of malware, from simple viruses to complex ransomware, and even mimic the evolving behavior of advanced persistent threats (APTs).[17]

In producing convincing network traffic patterns, AI can analyze large volumes of normal and anomalous network data to generate realistic traffic flows that include both benign activities and simulated attack patterns.[18] This capability is invaluable for training scenarios that focus on network monitoring and intrusion detection. The AI can create complex scenarios that include subtle indicators of compromise

---

[16] Fezari, Mohamed, Ali Al-Dahoud, and Ahmed Al-Dahoud. "Augmanting Reality: The Power of Generative AI." *University Badji Mokhtar Annaba: Annaba, Algeria* (2023).

[17] Sharma, Amit, et al. "Advanced persistent threats (apt): evolution, anatomy, attribution and countermeasures." *Journal of Ambient Intelligence and Humanized Computing* 14.7 (2023): 9355–9381.

[18] Alfawareh, Mohammad Daham. *Cyber Threat Intelligence Using Deep Learning to Detect Abnormal Network Behavior*. MS thesis. Princess Sumaya University for Technology (Jordan), 2020.

hidden within seemingly normal traffic, challenging trainees to identify and respond to potential threats as they would in real-world situations.

Implementing these AI-driven solutions for creating believable digital artifacts can be relatively straightforward for organizations with existing AI infrastructure and expertise. Many commercial cybersecurity training platforms now offer AI-generated content as part of their services, making it accessible even to organizations without in-house AI capabilities. These platforms often provide user-friendly interfaces for customizing scenarios and generating relevant artifacts, allowing for quick integration into existing training programs.

This sounds ideal; however, the implementation can be challenging for organizations looking to develop these capabilities in-house or those requiring highly specialized or sensitive scenarios. Challenges include the need for large, high-quality datasets to train the AI models effectively, which can be difficult to obtain, especially for simulating cutting-edge or industry-specific threats. There's also the complexity of developing and maintaining sophisticated AI models that can generate diverse and evolving artifacts. Additionally, ensuring that the generated content remains relevant and up-to-date with the latest threat landscapes requires ongoing effort and expertise. Despite these challenges, the benefits of AI-generated artifacts in cybersecurity training—including increased realism, scalability, and adaptability—make it a valuable investment for organizations committed to robust cybersecurity preparedness.

Creating believable digital artifacts for cybersecurity training, a diverse range of data sources can be leveraged. For generating realistic phishing emails, sources such as anonymized corporate email datasets, public email collections, phishing email databases, social media posts, and company websites provide valuable input. These sources offer insights into legitimate business communication styles, current phishing trends, and organizational language that can be mimicked in training scenarios. When it comes to simulating malware behavior and signatures, resources like malware databases (e.g., VirusTotal), cybersecurity reports, threat intelligence feeds, open-source malware code repositories, sandbox environment logs, and academic research papers on malware analysis are invaluable. These sources provide detailed information on malware structure, functionality, and the latest trends in malicious software.

For producing convincing network traffic patterns, data can be drawn from anonymized network logs of real organizations, public network datasets, simulated network environments, cybersecurity incident reports, network protocol specifications, and IoT device traffic patterns. These sources help in creating realistic baseline network activity and accurately simulating attack patterns.[19] It's crucial to note that when using these data sources, organizations must ensure compliance with privacy regulations and ethical guidelines. Many of these sources, especially those

---

[19] Bansal, Bijender, et al. "Big data architecture for network security." *Cyber Security and Network Security* (2022): 233–267.

4.3 Enhancing Realism Through AI-Generated Elements

containing sensitive or personal information, need to be carefully anonymized and sanitized before use.

The challenge in utilizing these data sources lies not just in their acquisition but in effectively integrating and processing them to train AI models. This requires significant expertise in data science, cybersecurity, and AI/machine learning, along with robust data management and AI training infrastructure. Organizations need to invest in these areas to handle the diverse and often large datasets effectively. Furthermore, to keep training scenarios current and relevant, there needs to be a continuous process of updating these data sources and retraining the AI models, which is particularly important given the rapidly evolving landscape of cybersecurity threats.

While compiling and utilizing these data sources is a complex task, the resulting ability to generate highly realistic and diverse training scenarios makes it a valuable endeavor for organizations committed to advanced cybersecurity training. The integration of such comprehensive and up-to-date data sources into AI-driven training systems can significantly enhance the realism and effectiveness of cybersecurity education, better preparing professionals for the challenges they may face in real-world scenarios.

Let's go over another hypothetical example to help bridge the gap between theory and practice. IN this scenario, let's examine how organizations of different sizes implement AI-powered cybersecurity training focused on creating believable digital artifacts. First, a small local credit union with 50 employees opts for a cloud-based AI training platform specialized in financial sector threats. The system generates tailored phishing emails mimicking local events, simulates common banking trojans in a safe environment, and produces simplified network traffic logs indicating potential data exfiltration attempts. This solution allows the credit union to provide relevant, industry-specific training without in-house AI expertise, helping employees identify phishing attempts and understand basic threat indicators.

On the other hand, a medium-sized regional hospital with 500 beds implements a more comprehensive AI-driven program to protect patient data and critical systems. The AI generates convincing phishing emails using hospital communication templates and current healthcare topics, simulates ransomware behavior targeting medical record systems, and produces complex network traffic patterns that include normal hospital operations interspersed with subtle anomalies. This approach enables hospital staff to become proficient in identifying sophisticated, healthcare-specific cyber threats, while the IT team gains valuable experience in detecting and mitigating attacks that could compromise patient care or data.

For a large multinational manufacturing corporation with 50,000 employees across multiple countries, the AI-driven cybersecurity training program is even more extensive. The system generates multi-lingual phishing campaigns targeting different departments with contextually relevant content, creates simulations of advanced persistent threats (APTs) targeting industrial control systems, and produces vast amounts of simulated network data reflecting global operations with embedded subtle indicators of various cyber threats. This comprehensive approach allows the organization to achieve a high level of cybersecurity preparedness across its diverse workforce, with the global security operations center gaining experience in detecting and managing complex, multi-vector attacks that could impact different aspects of the business.

In each case, the AI-powered system enables the creation of highly realistic and relevant training scenarios without exposing the organizations to actual risks. The scalability of the AI solution means that while the complexity and scope differ based on organizational size and needs, each entity can provide its employees with tailored, effective cybersecurity training that reflects its specific threat landscape. An approach like this can significantly enhance the ability of organizations, regardless of their size, to prepare their workforce for the evolving challenges of cybersecurity in their respective industries.

4.3.2 Simulating Human Behavior in Threat Scenarios

The capability of enhancing the creation of believable digital artifacts does have its benefits besides creating misinformation. There are ways that this can better society, one of which is developing realistic cybersecurity training environments that accurately reflect the complexities of human interactions in security situations. To model user interactions and responses, AI can be fed with data from various sources, including anonymized logs of user behavior during actual security incidents, survey responses on security practices, and simulated user interactions. This data allows the AI to generate a range of realistic user behaviors, from those who diligently follow security protocols to those who might inadvertently compromise security through carelessness or lack of awareness.

In terms of replicating attacker tactics and techniques, AI can be trained on datasets of known attack patterns, threat intelligence reports, and even information from ethical hacking communities. This enables the AI to simulate sophisticated attack scenarios that evolve in response to defensive actions, much like a real attacker would.[20] Generative AI can create dynamic attack narratives that adapt to the trainee's responses, providing a more engaging and realistic training experience.

Simulating organizational dynamics and policies is perhaps the most complex aspect. Here, AI can be fed with information about typical corporate structures, common security policies, and case studies of how organizations have responded to security incidents. This allows the AI to create believable scenarios that include elements like inter-departmental communication, policy enforcement, and decision-making processes during a security crisis.

Implementing such a system would vary in difficulty depending on the scale and sophistication desired. For basic implementations, off-the-shelf AI solutions could be adapted relatively easily, especially for smaller organizations with less complex needs. However, creating a highly sophisticated system that accurately simulates

---

[20] Hoffman, Wyatt. "AI and the Future of Cyber Competition." *CSET Issue Brief* (2021): 1–35.

4.3 Enhancing Realism Through AI-Generated Elements

the nuances of human behavior and organizational dynamics in diverse threat scenarios would be significantly more challenging. It would require substantial expertise in AI, cybersecurity, and behavioral psychology, as well as access to large, high-quality datasets. Additionally, ensuring that the simulations remain relevant and up-to-date with evolving threat landscapes and organizational practices would necessitate ongoing maintenance and updates.

The importance of implementing such measures cannot be overstated. Traditional cybersecurity training often fails to capture the human element of security threats, which is frequently the weakest link in an organization's defenses. By simulating realistic human behaviors and organizational dynamics, AI-powered training can provide a much more effective preparation for real-world scenarios. It allows cybersecurity professionals to practice not just technical skills, but also critical soft skills like communication, decision-making under pressure, and navigating complex organizational structures during a crisis. This holistic approach to training can significantly enhance an organization's overall security posture, helping to build a more resilient and prepared workforce capable of responding effectively to the diverse and evolving landscape of cyber threats.

To create believable digital artifacts and simulate human behavior in threat scenarios, a diverse array of data sources can be leveraged. These sources provide the essential foundation for AI models to generate realistic simulations across various aspects of cybersecurity training. For modeling user interactions and responses, data can be drawn from anonymized SIEM logs, employee surveys on security awareness, simulated user interaction data from existing training programs, and academic studies on human behavior in cybersecurity contexts. To replicate attacker tactics and techniques, valuable sources include threat intelligence feeds, open-source intelligence on known attack patterns, data from honeypot systems, incident response reports, and datasets from ethical hacking competitions. Simulating organizational dynamics and policies can be achieved by utilizing anonymized corporate policy documents, case studies of security incident responses, regulatory compliance guidelines, and research on organizational behavior during crises.

Additional general sources such as public datasets on human-computer interaction, social media data, and news articles about cybersecurity incidents can provide broader context and enhance the realism of simulations. It's crucial to note that when using these data sources, strict adherence to data protection regulations and ethical guidelines is paramount. Personal information must be thoroughly anonymized, and sensitive data handled with appropriate security measures to ensure privacy and compliance. The challenge in utilizing these data sources lies not just in their acquisition but in their effective integration and preprocessing to train AI models. This requires significant expertise in data science, cybersecurity, and AI/machine learning, along with substantial investments in data management infrastructure and AI training capabilities. Organizations need to be prepared to handle these diverse datasets effectively and continuously update them to keep simulations current and relevant in the face of rapidly evolving cyber threats and organizational practices.

While compiling and utilizing these data sources is undoubtedly a complex task,[21] the resulting ability to generate highly realistic and diverse training scenarios makes it an invaluable endeavor. The integration of such comprehensive data into AI-driven training systems can significantly enhance the realism and effectiveness of cybersecurity education. This approach better prepares professionals for the challenges they may face in real-world scenarios, ultimately strengthening an organization's overall cybersecurity posture.

Again, let's consider a hypothetical scenario where three organizations of different sizes implement AI-powered cybersecurity training focused on simulating human behavior in threat scenarios. As we did earlier, let's start off with a smaller organization and examine different organization sizes and how this could apply to them. For example, a small local accounting firm with 25 employees opts for a cloud-based AI training platform specialized in financial sector threats. The system generates scenarios that model typical user interactions within a small office environment, such as simulating an employee accidentally opening a malicious email attachment or falling for a phone-based social engineering attack. The AI replicates attacker tactics by creating convincing phishing emails and simulated phone calls that mimic common threats to accounting firms. Organizational dynamics are simulated through scenarios that involve decision-making processes typical in a small business, like how to respond when a potential data breach is discovered. This solution allows the firm to provide relevant, industry-specific training without in-house AI expertise, helping employees understand how their actions impact overall security.

A medium-sized regional hospital with 500 beds implements a more comprehensive AI-driven program. The system models a wide range of user interactions, from nurses accessing patient records to administrators handling sensitive financial data. It simulates sophisticated attacker techniques targeting healthcare systems, such as ransomware attacks on medical devices or attempts to steal patient data. The AI also replicates complex organizational dynamics, including scenarios that involve coordinating responses across different departments during a security incident. This approach enables hospital staff to practice responding to realistic threats while navigating the unique challenges of maintaining patient care and privacy in a healthcare setting.

For a large multinational tech company with 50,000 employees across multiple countries, the AI-driven cybersecurity training program is extensive and highly sophisticated. The system models diverse user behaviors across various roles and cultural contexts, simulating how employees in different countries might respond to security threats. It replicates advanced attacker tactics, including nation-state level cyber espionage attempts targeting the company's intellectual property. The AI simulates complex organizational dynamics, including scenarios that involve coordinating global incident response teams, managing public relations during a

---

[21] Elish, Madeleine Clare, and Danah Boyd. "Situating methods in the magic of Big Data and AI." *Communication monographs* 85.1 (2018): 57–80.

high-profile breach, and navigating differing international data protection regulations. This comprehensive approach allows the company to prepare its diverse workforce for a wide range of potential security scenarios, enhancing its global security posture.

In each case, the AI-powered system enables the creation of highly realistic and relevant training scenarios tailored to the specific needs and context of each organization. While the complexity and scope differ based on organizational size and needs, each entity can provide its employees with effective cybersecurity training that reflects its unique threat landscape and organizational structure. This approach significantly enhances the ability of organizations, regardless of their size, to prepare their workforce for the complex, human-centric challenges of modern cybersecurity.

4.4 Measuring and Improving Scenario Effectiveness

This section focuses on the critical aspects of evaluating and enhancing the effectiveness of AI-generated cybersecurity training scenarios. It explores methods for analyzing learner performance and engagement, including tracking key performance indicators, identifying common mistakes and misconceptions, and assessing the transfer of learning to real-world situations. The section also delves into the continuous refinement process for AI-generated scenarios, discussing the incorporation of learner feedback, adaptation to evolving cybersecurity landscapes, and optimization of scenario difficulty and complexity. Consequently, by examining these measurement and improvement strategies, this section highlights how AI-driven training can be iteratively enhanced to provide increasingly effective and relevant cybersecurity education.

4.4.1 Analyzing Learner Performance and Engagement

Analyzing learner performance and engagement is a crucial aspect of AI-powered cybersecurity training, allowing for continuous improvement and personalization of the learning experience. Tracking Key Performance Indicators (KPIs) such as completion rates, time spent on modules, and success rates in simulated scenarios enables organizations to gain valuable insights into the effectiveness of their training programs.[22] AI algorithms can process this data to identify trends and patterns, helping to pinpoint areas where the training is most effective and where it may need improvement. Furthermore, this analysis can help in tailoring the training content to

---

[22] Chowdhury, Nabin, Sokratis Katsikas, and Vasileios Gkioulos. "Modeling effective cybersecurity training frameworks: A delphi method-based study." *Computers & Security* 113 (2022): 102551.

individual learners, ensuring that each participant receives the most relevant and challenging material based on their performance.

Identifying common mistakes and misconceptions is another vital aspect of this analysis. AI systems can aggregate data[23] from numerous training sessions to highlight recurring errors or misunderstandings among learners. This information is invaluable for refining training content, addressing specific knowledge gaps, and developing targeted interventions to correct these misconceptions. Additionally, by analyzing patterns in learner responses, AI can help identify potential blind spots in an organization's overall security awareness, allowing for proactive measures to be taken before these weaknesses can be exploited in real-world situations.

Assessing the transfer of learning to real-world situations is perhaps the most critical and challenging aspect of measuring training effectiveness. AI can assist in this by correlating training performance with actual security incident data within an organization. For instance, if phishing attempt success rates decrease following specific training modules, it provides tangible evidence of the training's impact. AI can also simulate complex, evolving scenarios that mimic real-world situations, allowing for a more accurate assessment of how well learners can apply their knowledge in practice.

While the benefits of such comprehensive analysis are significant, they come with extensive challenges, particularly in terms of data privacy and security. The EU AI Act[24] classifies AI systems used in educational settings as high-risk, requiring stringent compliance measures. Similarly, the Colorado AI Act and the FTC's enforcement actions on AI usage emphasize the need for transparency, fairness, and robust data protection. Organizations must ensure that all data collected during training is anonymized, securely stored, and used only for its intended purpose. This includes implementing strong cybersecurity practices to prevent breaches or unauthorized access to this sensitive information, which could potentially reveal individual performance metrics or organizational vulnerabilities.

The aggregation of this data across organizations or industries could provide invaluable insights into cybersecurity training effectiveness and trends. However, this also presents additional challenges in terms of data sharing agreements, potential competitive concerns, and the need for even more robust anonymization techniques to prevent the identification of individuals or specific organizations. Balancing the potential benefits of such aggregated analysis with the privacy and security risks requires careful consideration and the implementation of advanced data protection measures.

---

[23] Kitaguchi, Daichi, and Masaaki Ito. "The power of AI on aggregating, managing, and curating medical knowledge for global surgical education." *Global Surgical Education-Journal of the Association for Surgical Education* 3.1 (2024): 1–7.

[24] Smuha, Nathalie A., et al. "How the EU can achieve legally trustworthy AI: a response to the European Commission's proposal for an Artificial Intelligence Act." *Available at SSRN 3899991* (2021).

4.4.2 Continuous Refinement of AI-Generated Scenarios

Continuous refinement of AI-generated scenarios is crucial for maintaining the effectiveness and relevance of cybersecurity training programs.[25] Incorporating learner feedback is a key component of this process. AI systems can analyze both explicit feedback (such as surveys and ratings) and implicit feedback (such as engagement levels and performance metrics) to understand how learners are interacting with the scenarios. This data can be used to identify areas where scenarios are too easy, too difficult, or not engaging enough. The AI can then automatically adjust these scenarios or suggest improvements to human trainers. For example, if many learners consistently struggle with a particular aspect of a phishing simulation, the AI might adjust the difficulty or provide additional context to improve learning outcomes.

Adapting to changing cybersecurity landscapes is another critical aspect of scenario refinement. The threat landscape in cybersecurity is constantly evolving, with new attack vectors and techniques emerging regularly. AI systems can be designed to continuously ingest and analyze data from various sources such as threat intelligence feeds, security bulletins, and recent incident reports. This allows the AI to dynamically update and create new scenarios that reflect the latest threats and vulnerabilities. For instance, if a new type of ransomware begins targeting a specific industry, the AI can quickly generate training scenarios that simulate this threat, ensuring that learners are prepared for current real-world risks.

Optimizing scenario difficulty and complexity is essential for maintaining learner engagement and ensuring effective skill development. AI can analyze individual learner performance data to dynamically adjust the difficulty and complexity of scenarios on a per-user basis. This could involve gradually increasing the sophistication of simulated attacks as a learner's skills improve, or introducing more nuanced scenarios that require the application of multiple cybersecurity concepts simultaneously. The AI can also identify when learners are ready to be challenged with more complex, multi-stage scenarios that more closely mimic advanced persistent threats or elaborate social engineering campaigns. This personalized approach ensures that each learner is consistently challenged at an appropriate level, maximizing their learning potential and maintaining their engagement with the training program.

Subsequently, continuously refining scenarios in these ways, AI-powered cybersecurity training can remain highly relevant, engaging, and effective. This adaptive approach allows organizations to maintain a well-prepared workforce capable of facing the ever-changing landscape of cyber threats. However, it's important to note that this level of refinement requires sophisticated AI systems, access to up-to-date threat intelligence, and careful balancing to ensure that the training remains aligned with organizational goals and compliance requirements. Regular human oversight

---

[25] Familoni, Babajide Tolulope. "Cybersecurity challenges in the age of AI: theoretical approaches and practical solutions." *Computer Science & IT Research Journal* 5.3 (2024): 703–724.

and input from cybersecurity experts remain crucial to guide the AI's refinement process and ensure the scenarios remain realistic and valuable for learners. Remember—AI isn't here to replace us, it's here to augment our capabilities and if we harness it correctly, create a safer digital future.

4.5 Ethical Considerations in AI-Generated Threat Scenarios

Given our last statement in 4.4, it is prudent that we address ethical considerations in AI-generated threat scenarios. This section addresses the crucial ethical considerations in designing and implementing AI-generated threat scenarios for cybersecurity training. It explores the importance of responsible scenario design, focusing on avoiding harmful or overly stressful content, maintaining privacy and data protection, and addressing potential biases in AI-generated material. The section also examines the delicate balance between realism and learner well-being, discussing strategies for providing adequate support and debriefing, establishing clear boundaries between training and reality, and promoting a positive learning environment. Thus, by highlighting these ethical aspects, this section emphasizes the importance of creating effective yet responsible AI-driven cybersecurity training experiences that prioritize both educational value and participant welfare.

4.5.1 Ensuring Responsible Scenario Design

Ensuring responsible scenario design is paramount in AI-powered cybersecurity training to create effective, ethical, and safe learning experiences. This involves carefully considering the content, privacy implications, and potential biases in AI-generated scenarios.[26] Harmful or overly stressful content in cybersecurity training could include scenarios that are excessively graphic or emotionally distressing. For example, a simulated ransomware attack that threatens to release sensitive personal information of employees or patients in a healthcare setting could be unnecessarily stressful. Similarly, scenarios involving extreme consequences such as simulated loss of life due to a cyber-attack on critical infrastructure could be too intense for learners. While realism is important, it's crucial to avoid content that could traumatize participants or create undue anxiety about their responsibilities.

---

[26] Kaushik, Keshav, et al. "Ethical Considerations in AI-Based Cybersecurity." *Next-Generation Cybersecurity: AI, ML, and Blockchain*. Singapore: Springer Nature Singapore, 2024. 437–470.

4.5 Ethical Considerations in AI-Generated Threat Scenarios

Maintaining privacy and data protection in AI-powered training scenarios requires multiple approaches.[27] One technique is data anonymization,[28] where any real-world data used to train the AI or create scenarios is stripped of personally identifiable information. Another tactic is using synthetic data generation, where the AI creates entirely fictional but realistic data sets for training purposes.[29] Implementing strict access controls and encryption for any data used in or generated by the training system is also crucial. Additionally, establishing clear data retention and deletion policies ensures that any information collected during training sessions is handled responsibly and disposed of appropriately.

Addressing potential biases in AI-generated content is a complex but essential task. Biases could manifest in various ways, such as scenarios disproportionately featuring certain types of attacks, consistently portraying specific demographics as attackers or victims, or reflecting outdated stereotypes about technology users. To address these biases, it's important to regularly audit the AI's outputs for patterns of bias and to diversify the data sets used to train the AI. Implementing human oversight in the scenario creation process can help catch and correct biases that the AI might introduce. Moreover, fostering diverse representation in the team developing the AI and designing the training programs can bring different perspectives and help identify potential biases. Continuously gathering feedback from a diverse group of learners and cybersecurity professionals can also provide insights into any biases that may not be immediately apparent to the development team.

4.5.2 Balancing Realism with Learner Well-Being

Balancing realism with learner well-being is crucial in AI-powered cybersecurity training to ensure effective learning without causing undue stress or anxiety. This balance requires careful consideration of support mechanisms, clear boundaries, and the overall learning environment. Providing adequate support involves multiple strategies. First, ensuring that learners have access to mentors or instructors who can offer guidance and answer questions throughout the training process is essential. This could be implemented through regular check-ins, office hours, or a dedicated support channel. Additionally, providing comprehensive resources such as reference materials, FAQs, and troubleshooting guides can help learners feel supported as they navigate complex scenarios. It's also important to have mental health

---

[27] Vegesna, Vinod Varma. "Privacy-Preserving Techniques in AI-Powered Cyber Security: Challenges and Opportunities." *International Journal of Machine Learning for Sustainable Development* 5.4 (2023): 1–8.

[28] Yang, Le, et al. "AI-Driven Anonymization: Protecting Personal Data Privacy While Leveraging Machine Learning." *arXiv preprint arXiv:2402.17191* (2024).

[29] Kishore, Aman, et al. "Synthetic data generation using imitation training." *Proceedings of the IEEE/CVF International Conference on Computer Vision.* 2021.

resources available, recognizing that some simulations may be stressful or emotionally challenging.

Debriefing is a critical component of the learning process and serves several purposes. It allows learners to process their experiences, reflect on their decisions, and understand the consequences of their actions in a safe environment.[30] Effective debriefing methods include group discussions, individual reflection exercises, and structured feedback sessions. These sessions should focus not only on what happened during the simulation but also on why certain decisions were made and what could be done differently in the future. Debriefing is important because it helps consolidate learning, reduces stress by providing closure, and allows learners to connect their training experiences to real-world applications.

Establishing clear boundaries between training and reality is crucial to prevent unnecessary anxiety and maintain a healthy perspective. This can be achieved by clearly labeling all training materials and scenarios as simulations, using distinct visual cues or interfaces for training environments, and regularly reminding participants that they are in a safe, controlled learning situation. It's important to emphasize that mistakes made during training are opportunities for learning, not real-world failures. Organizations should also have clear policies about when and how training scenarios can be conducted to avoid confusion with real incidents. If learners feel their well-being is being affected, they should have clear pathways for seeking help. This could include speaking with their direct supervisor, contacting the Human Resources department, or reaching out to designated mental health professionals or employee assistance programs. It's crucial that these support options are communicated clearly and that seeking help is encouraged and destigmatized within the organization.

A positive learning environment[31] in cybersecurity training is characterized by open communication, mutual respect, and a focus on growth rather than perfection. It encourages questions, values diverse perspectives, and celebrates progress. To create this environment, organizations can foster a culture of continuous learning, provide opportunities for peer collaboration and support, and ensure that feedback is constructive and growth-oriented. Regular surveys or feedback sessions can help gauge the learning environment's effectiveness and identify areas for improvement. Additionally, recognizing and rewarding not just successful outcomes but also effort, creativity, and teamwork can contribute to a positive atmosphere. By prioritizing learner well-being alongside realistic training, organizations can create a robust, effective, and sustainable cybersecurity training program.

---

[30] Angafor, Giddeon N., Iryna Yevseyeva, and Ying He. "Game-based learning: A review of tabletop exercises for cybersecurity incident response training." *Security and privacy* 3.6 (2020): e126.

[31] Hue, Ming-tak, and Wai-shing Li. *Classroom management: Creating a positive learning environment*. Vol. 1. Hong Kong University Press, 2008.

References

1. Shivapurkar, M., Bhatia, S., & Ahmed, I. (2020). Problem-based learning for cybersecurity education. *Journal of the Colloquium for Information Systems Security Education, 7*(1).
2. Chen, L., Chen, P., & Lin, Z. (2020). Artificial intelligence in education: A review. *IEEE Access, 8*, 75264–75278.
3. Kallonas, C., Piki, A., & Stavrou, E. (2024). Empowering professionals: A generative AI approach to personalized cybersecurity learning. In *2024 IEEE global engineering education conference (EDUCON)*. IEEE.
4. Bécue, A., Praça, I., & Gama, J. (2021). Artificial intelligence, cyber-threats and industry 4.0: Challenges and opportunities. *Artificial Intelligence Review, 54*(5), 3849–3886.
5. Loaiza, F. L., et al. (2019). *Utility of artificial intelligence and machine learning in cybersecurity*. Institute for Defense Analyses.
6. Montasari, R., et al. (2021). Application of artificial intelligence and machine learning in producing actionable cyber threat intelligence. In *Digital forensic investigation of internet of things (IoT) devices* (pp. 47–64).
7. Khodaiemehr, H., Bagheri, K., & Feng, C. (2023). Navigating the quantum computing threat landscape for blockchains: A comprehensive survey. *Authorea Preprints*.
8. Sarker, I. H. (2024). AI for critical infrastructure protection and resilience. In *AI-driven cybersecurity and threat intelligence: Cyber automation, intelligent decision-making and explainability* (pp. 153–172).
9. Singh, S., et al. (2020). Artificial intelligence and security of industrial control systems. In *Handbook of Big Data Privacy* (pp. 121–164).
10. Yeng, P. K., et al. (2021). Data-driven and artificial intelligence (AI) approach for modelling and analyzing healthcare security practice: a systematic review. In *Intelligent systems and applications: Proceedings of the 2020 intelligent systems conference (IntelliSys)* (Vol. 1). Springer.
11. Dash, A., Ye, J., & Wang, G. (2023). A review of generative adversarial networks (GANs) and its applications in a wide variety of disciplines: From medical to remote sensing. *IEEE Access*.
12. Ivanovic, B., et al. (2020). Multimodal deep generative models for trajectory prediction: A conditional variational autoencoder approach. *IEEE Robotics and Automation Letters, 6*(2), 295–302.
13. Hassanin, M., & Moustafa, N. (2024). A comprehensive overview of Large Language Models (LLMs) for cyber defences: Opportunities and directions. *arXiv preprint arXiv, 2405*, 14487.
14. Li, Z., et al. (2021). A survey of convolutional neural networks: Analysis, applications, and prospects. *IEEE Transactions on Neural Networks and Learning Systems, 33*(12), 6999–7019.
15. Fezari, M., Al-Dahoud, A., & Al-Dahoud, A. (2023). *Augmanting reality: The power of generative AI*. University Badji Mokhtar Annaba.
16. Sharma, A., et al. (2023). Advanced persistent threats (apt): Evolution, anatomy, attribution and countermeasures. *Journal of Ambient Intelligence and Humanized Computing, 14*(7), 9355–9381.
17. Alfawareh, M. D. (2020). *Cyber threat intelligence using deep learning to detect abnormal network behavior*. MS thesis. Princess Sumaya University for Technology (Jordan).
18. Bansal, B., et al. (2022). Big data architecture for network security. *Cyber Security and Network Security*, 233–267.
19. Hoffman, W. (2021). AI and the future of cyber competition. *CSET Issue Brief*, 1–35.
20. Elish, M. C., & Boyd, D. (2018). Situating methods in the magic of big data and AI. *Communication Monographs, 85*(1), 57–80.
21. Chowdhury, N., Katsikas, S., & Gkioulos, V. (2022). Modeling effective cybersecurity training frameworks: A delphi method-based study. *Computers & Security, 113*, 102551.
22. Kitaguchi, D., & Ito, M. (2024). The power of AI on aggregating, managing, and curating medical knowledge for global surgical education. *Global Surgical Education-Journal of the Association for Surgical Education, 3*(1), 1–7.

23. Smuha, N. A., et al. (2021). *How the EU can achieve legally trustworthy AI: A response to the European Commission's proposal for an Artificial Intelligence Act.* Available at SSRN 3899991.
24. Familoni, B. T. (2024). Cybersecurity challenges in the age of AI: Theoretical approaches and practical solutions. *Computer Science & IT Research Journal, 5*(3), 703–724.
25. Kaushik, K., et al. (2024). Ethical considerations in AI-based cybersecurity. In *Next-generation cybersecurity: AI, ML, and Blockchain* (pp. 437–470). Springer.
26. Vegesna, V. V. (2023). Privacy-preserving techniques in AI-powered cyber security: Challenges and opportunities. *International Journal of Machine Learning for Sustainable Development, 5*(4), 1–8.
27. Yang, L., et al. (2024). AI-driven anonymization: Protecting personal data privacy while leveraging machine learning. *arXiv preprint arXiv, 2402*, 17191.
28. Kishore, A., et al. (2021). Synthetic data generation using imitation training. In *Proceedings of the IEEE/CVF International Conference on Computer Vision.*
29. Angafor, G. N., Yevseyeva, I., & He, Y. (2020). Game-based learning: A review of tabletop exercises for cybersecurity incident response training. *Security and Privacy, 3*(6), e126.

Chapter 5
AI-Enhanced Virtual and Augmented Reality for Cybersecurity Training

This chapter explores the integration of AI with virtual reality (VR) and augmented reality (AR) technologies to create immersive and interactive cybersecurity training experiences. This chapter delves into the cutting-edge intersection of artificial intelligence, virtual reality (VR), and augmented reality (AR) in the realm of cybersecurity training. This chapter explores how these technologies combine to create immersive, interactive, and highly effective learning experiences for cybersecurity professionals. Thus, examining the potential of VR and AR in providing realistic environments and hands-on practice, the chapter showcases how AI-driven enhancements can revolutionize training methodologies. It covers intelligent interaction mechanisms, adaptive challenges, and automated assessments, while also addressing the crucial aspects of designing effective training modules. Additionally, the chapter highlights the importance of balancing realism with usability and integrates a discussion on the security risks inherent in VR and AR technologies, including recent incidents that underscore the need for vigilance in this rapidly evolving field.

5.1 The Potential of VR and AR in Cybersecurity Training

This section explores the transformative potential of Virtual Reality (VR) and Augmented Reality (AR) in cybersecurity training. By providing realistic and engaging learning environments, VR and AR technologies offer unprecedented opportunities for immersive experiences that closely mirror real-world scenarios. From simulated Security Operations Centers to virtual network infrastructures and AR-enhanced physical security training, these technologies create a rich, interactive learning landscape. Furthermore, this section delves into how VR and AR enable hands-on practice and skill development, offering virtual labs for ethical hacking, AR-assisted hardware troubleshooting, and collaborative VR environments for team exercises. Through these applications, VR and AR are revolutionizing the way cybersecurity professionals acquire and hone their skills, bridging the gap between theoretical knowledge and practical experience in a safe, controlled, yet remarkably realistic virtual environment.

5.1.1 Providing Realistic and Engaging Learning Environments

The integration of VR and AR with AI can significantly enhance cybersecurity training by providing highly realistic and engaging learning environments.[1] For Security Operations Centers (SOCs), VR can create immersive simulations that replicate the look, feel, and functionality of actual SOC environments. Trainees can interact with virtual workstations, multiple screens displaying real-time data feeds, and simulated alert systems. AI can generate dynamic scenarios, mimicking the unpredictable nature of cyber threats, while adapting the complexity based on the trainee's performance. This approach allows cybersecurity professionals to experience the pressure and decision-making challenges of a SOC without the risks associated with real-world operations.

Virtual network infrastructure and attack scenarios in VR can provide a safe yet realistic environment for trainees to practice defending against various cyber threats. AI can simulate complex network topologies and generate diverse attack vectors, from DDoS attacks to sophisticated APTs.[2] Trainees can navigate through virtual server rooms, interact with network devices, and respond to incidents in real-time. The AI can dynamically adjust the scenario, introducing new challenges or altering attack patterns based on the trainee's actions, providing a deeply engaging and responsive training experience.

AR can be particularly effective for physical security training, overlaying[3] digital information onto the real world. For example, trainees wearing AR glasses could walk through an actual office space and see virtual indicators of potential security vulnerabilities, such as unsecured workstations or unauthorized devices. Meta's smart glasses[4] and Quest[5] would be examples of devices that could serve the aforementioned purposes.

AI can generate these scenarios, adapting them to the specific layout and security concerns of different environments. This approach bridges the gap between

---

[1] Wagner, Paul, and Dalal Alharthi. "Leveraging VR/AR/MR/XR Technologies to Improve Cybersecurity Education, Training, and Operations." *Journal of Cybersecurity Education, Research and Practice* 2024.1 (2023): 7.

[2] Myneni, Sowmya. *Defeating Attackers by Bridging the Gaps Between Security and Intelligence*. Arizona State University, 2022.

[3] Rampolla, Joseph, and Greg Kipper. *Augmented reality: An emerging technologies guide to AR*. Elsevier, 2012.

[4] Smart Glasses Made Smarter with Meta AI. Meta. https://www.meta.com/smart-glasses

[5] This Is Meta Quest. Meta. https://www.meta.com/quest

cybersecurity and physical security training, helping professionals understand the interconnected nature of modern security challenges.

Implementing such VR/AR training systems integrated with AI requires careful consideration of several factors. First, there's the need for high-quality VR/AR hardware and software capable of rendering realistic environments without causing discomfort or disorientation, as discussed in Chap. 4. The AI systems must be sophisticated enough to generate believable scenarios and adapt in real-time to trainee actions. Data privacy and security are crucial considerations, especially when simulating realistic network environments or using actual office layouts for AR training, also addressed extensively in Chap. 4. Organizations must also consider the initial cost of implementation and ongoing maintenance of these systems. Despite these challenges, the potential for improved learning outcomes is significant. This immersive approach can lead to better retention of knowledge, improved decision-making skills under pressure, and increased confidence in handling real-world scenarios.

For SOC training specifically, VR/AR integrated with AI can simulate a wide range of capabilities and scenarios. Trainees can practice monitoring and responding to various types of alerts, from low-level anomalies to critical security breaches. They can interact with simulated Intrusion Detection/Prevention Systems (IDS/IPS), analyzing and responding to potential intrusions in real-time. The training can include scenarios involving firewall configuration and management, allowing trainees to see the immediate impact of their decisions on network security. Authentication and authorization challenges can be simulated, requiring trainees to manage access controls and identify potential insider threats. Thus, providing hands-on experience with these diverse aspects of SOC operations, VR/AR training can help prepare cybersecurity professionals more comprehensively for their roles. Subsequently, this could be revolutionizing for the cyber industry given the immense workforce shortage.

This type of immersive, realistic training can significantly help in addressing burnout in the cybersecurity field. Allowing professionals to practice handling high-stress situations in a safe environment, they can build confidence in their and develop effective coping strategies. For example, a trainee might experience a simulated major security breach, practicing their incident response skills without the real-world consequences. This can help reduce anxiety about handling such situations in reality. Additionally, the engaging nature of VR/AR training can make the learning process more enjoyable, potentially increasing job satisfaction and reducing burnout. As professionals feel better prepared and more confident in their skills, they may experience less stress and greater job satisfaction in their actual roles, potentially leading to reduced turnover in the high-pressure field of cybersecurity.

5.1.2 Enabling Hands-On Practice and Skill Development

The integration of AI with VR and AR technologies can significantly enhance hands-on practice and skill development in cybersecurity training,[6] particularly in areas like ethical hacking and penetration testing. For instance, consider a scenario where a healthcare software system is experiencing high levels of breaches and requires more robust defenses. A VR environment, powered by AI, could simulate this entire system, allowing ethical hackers to practice their skills in a realistic yet safe setting. The AI could generate a complex virtual network mirroring the healthcare system's architecture, complete with simulated patient data, various access points, and typical vulnerabilities found in healthcare IT infrastructures.

In this virtual environment, trainees could go through each step of the penetration testing process. During the reconnaissance phase, they could use virtual tools to scan the network, with the AI dynamically generating realistic network responses and potential entry points. As hackers move to the compromising phase, the AI could simulate various defense mechanisms, adapting in real-time to the hacker's attempts to exploit vulnerabilities. This could include simulating social engineering attacks on virtual staff members, attempting to breach firewalls, or exploiting software vulnerabilities. The AI could even introduce unexpected scenarios, such as a sudden patch update or a change in network configuration, forcing the ethical hackers to adapt their strategies on the fly. Throughout this process, VR provides an immersive experience, allowing hackers to 'physically' navigate through virtual server rooms or workstations, enhancing the realism of the exercise.

AR technology can be particularly effective in troubleshooting security hardware. Imagine a scenario where cybersecurity professionals need to diagnose and fix issues with physical security devices like firewalls or intrusion detection systems. Using AR glasses, trainees could see overlays of real-time diagnostic information when looking at the hardware. The AI could guide them through the troubleshooting process, highlighting potential issues, suggesting steps to take, and even simulating the outcomes of different actions before they're performed. This approach not only speeds up the learning process but also reduces the risk of causing actual damage to expensive equipment during training.

For team-based exercises, collaborative VR environments[7] powered by AI can create complex, multi-faceted scenarios that require coordination and communication among team members. For example, a simulated large-scale cyber attack could require different team members to take on various roles—some managing the immediate threat, others communicating with stakeholders, and others working on long-term solutions. The AI could dynamically adjust the scenario based on the

---

[6] Qawasmeh, Saif Al-Dean, Ali Abdullah S. AlQahtani, and Muhammad Khurram Khan. "Navigating Cybersecurity Training: A Comprehensive Review." *arXiv preprint arXiv:2401.11326* (2024).

[7] Churchill, Elizabeth F., David N. Snowdon, and Alan J. Munro, eds. *Collaborative virtual environments: digital places and spaces for interaction.* Springer Science & Business Media, 2012.

team's actions, introducing new challenges or altering the attack vector to test the team's adaptability and cooperation skills.

AI takes these training scenarios to the next level by introducing an unprecedented degree of realism, adaptability, and personalization. It can analyze each trainee's actions in real-time, adjusting the difficulty and focus of the exercises to address individual strengths and weaknesses. For instance, if a trainee consistently struggles with a particular type of vulnerability, the AI could generate more scenarios focusing on that area. Moreover, AI can simulate intelligent adversaries that learn and adapt to the strategies employed by the trainees, much like real-world attackers would. This level of dynamic interaction is simply not possible with traditional training methods.

The 'next level' of AI-enhanced VR/AR training could involve creating highly personalized, continuously evolving training environments. Imagine a system that not only adapts to individual trainees but also learns from the collective experiences of all users, constantly refining and updating its scenarios to reflect the latest real-world threats and best practices. It could even predict future potential attack vectors based on current trends and create speculative scenarios to prepare cybersecurity professionals for threats that don't yet exist but may emerge. This forward-looking approach could revolutionize cybersecurity training, moving it from a reactive to a proactive model, and significantly enhancing the industry's ability to stay ahead of cyber threats.

5.2 AI-Driven Enhancements in VR and AR Training

This section delves into the sophisticated ways artificial intelligence enhances VR and AR training in cybersecurity. It explores how AI drives intelligent interaction and feedback mechanisms, utilizing natural language processing for guidance and real-time analysis of learner actions to provide contextual support. The section also examines AI's role in creating adaptive difficulty and personalized challenges, dynamically adjusting scenario complexity and tailoring content to individual learning styles. Additionally, it covers the implementation of automated assessment and performance tracking, showcasing how AI-powered metrics and analytics can provide detailed insights into learner behavior and predict skill development trajectories. Through these AI-driven enhancements, VR and AR training experiences become more responsive, personalized, and effective, significantly elevating the quality and impact of cybersecurity education.

5.2.1 Intelligent Interaction and Feedback Mechanisms

AI integration in VR/AR cybersecurity training can significantly enhance the learning experience through intelligent interaction and feedback mechanisms. Natural Language Processing (NLP) can be used to create virtual assistant guidance, allowing trainees to interact with the training environment using natural language.[8] This enables a more intuitive and responsive learning experience, where trainees can ask questions, request help, or receive explanations in real-time. AI-powered real-time analysis of learner actions and decisions provides immediate and personalized feedback, helping trainees understand the consequences of their choices in complex cybersecurity scenarios. Furthermore, AI can offer contextual hints and suggestions based on performance, adapting the difficulty and focus of the training to each individual's learning pace and style.

For Natural Language Processing in virtual assistant guidance, imagine a scenario where a trainee is working on securing a virtual network in a VR environment. They can ask the AI assistant questions like, "What vulnerabilities should I look for in the firewall configuration?" The AI, understanding the context and the trainee's current task, could provide a detailed explanation, highlighting potential weak points and suggesting best practices for firewall setup. This natural interaction allows for a more fluid learning experience, mimicking real-world mentor-mentee relationships.

In terms of real-time analysis of learner actions and decisions, consider a scenario where a trainee is responding to a simulated ransomware attack in a VR environment. As the trainee takes actions like isolating affected systems or attempting to decrypt files, the AI continuously analyzes these decisions. It could provide immediate feedback on the effectiveness of each action, perhaps through a virtual heads-up display showing the impact on the spread of the ransomware or the potential data loss. This real-time feedback allows trainees to quickly understand the consequences of their decisions and adjust their strategies accordingly.

For contextual hints and suggestions based on performance, picture a trainee practicing penetration testing in an AR-enhanced environment. If the AI detects that the trainee is struggling to identify a particular vulnerability, it could offer a subtle hint by highlighting relevant areas in the AR overlay. For instance, if the trainee has overlooked an unsecured IoT device, the AI might cause it to glow slightly in the AR view, prompting the trainee to investigate further. As the trainee's skills improve, these hints would become more subtle or less frequent, ensuring that the challenge level remains appropriate to their developing expertise.

---

[8] Wang, Mengying, et al. "Intelligent virtual case learning system based on real medical records and natural language processing." *BMC Medical Informatics and Decision Making* 22.1 (2022): 60.

5.2.2 Adaptive Difficulty and Personalized Challenges

AI integration with AR/VR in cybersecurity training offers powerful capabilities for creating adaptive difficulty and personalized challenges. This combination allows for a highly responsive and tailored learning experience that can significantly enhance the effectiveness of cybersecurity education. By leveraging AI algorithms, the training system can dynamically adjust scenario complexity, tailor content to individual learning styles, and implement progression systems based on skill mastery.

Dynamic adjustment of scenario complexity is a key feature of AI-enhanced VR/AR training.[9] The AI can analyze a trainee's performance in real-time and adjust the difficulty of cybersecurity scenarios accordingly. For instance, if a trainee is excelling at detecting basic phishing attempts, the AI might introduce more sophisticated social engineering tactics or multi-vector attacks. Conversely, if a trainee is struggling with a particular concept, the AI can simplify the scenario or provide additional guidance. This ensures that each trainee is consistently challenged at an appropriate level, maintaining engagement and optimizing learning outcomes.

Tailoring training content to individual learning styles is another significant advantage of AI integration. Analyzing patterns in a trainee's interactions, performance, and preferences, enables AI to adapt the presentation of information to suit their learning style. For visual learners, the system might emphasize graphical representations of network architectures in VR. For those who learn best through hands-on experience, the AI could generate more interactive scenarios in AR that require physical manipulation of virtual objects. This personalization ensures that each trainee receives information in a format that resonates best with their cognitive preferences, enhancing comprehension and retention.

Progression systems based on skill mastery leverage AI to create a structured learning path that adapts to each trainee's rate of advancement.[10] The AI can track proficiency across various cybersecurity skills and concepts, unlocking new, more advanced scenarios as trainees demonstrate mastery. This gamified approach not only motivates learners by providing a sense of achievement but also ensures that they have a solid foundation before moving on to more complex topics. The AI can also identify areas where a trainee might need additional practice, automatically generating focused exercises to reinforce these skills.

To illustrate these concepts, let's consider some examples. For dynamic adjustment of scenario complexity, imagine a VR simulation of a Security Operations Center (SOC). A trainee begins by handling basic alert triage. As they demonstrate proficiency, the AI introduces more complex incidents, such as a sophisticated APT

---

[9] Papakostas, Christos, Christos Troussas, and Cleo Sgouropoulou. "Review of the Literature on AI-Enhanced Augmented Reality in Education." *Special Topics in Artificial Intelligence and Augmented Reality: The Case of Spatial Intelligence Enhancement* (2024): 13–50.

[10] Stanney, Kay M., et al. "Performance gains from adaptive eXtended Reality training fueled by artificial intelligence." *The Journal of Defense Modeling and Simulation* 19.2 (2022): 195–218.

attack that unfolds over time. The AI adjusts the scenario in real-time, perhaps introducing new attack vectors or changing the attacker's tactics based on the trainee's responses, ensuring a constantly challenging and engaging experience.

In tailoring content to learning styles, consider an AR training module on network security. For a trainee who shows a preference for visual learning, the AI might present network topologies as 3D holograms that the trainee can manipulate and explore. For another trainee who learns best through problem-solving, the same content might be presented as a series of interactive puzzles where they need to configure virtual routers and firewalls to secure the network.

For progression systems based on skill mastery,[11] envision a comprehensive VR cybersecurity training program. The AI tracks a trainee's performance across various domains like cryptography, network security, and incident response. As the trainee masters basic concepts in each area, they unlock more advanced scenarios. For instance, after demonstrating proficiency in basic encryption techniques, the trainee might unlock a challenging scenario involving quantum cryptography and its implications for future security protocols.

These AI-driven approaches in VR/AR training environments provide a level of personalization and adaptivity that traditional training methods cannot match. They ensure that each trainee receives a uniquely tailored, consistently challenging, and highly engaging learning experience, ultimately producing more skilled and confident cybersecurity professionals.

5.2.3 Automated Assessment and Performance Tracking

Automated assessment and performance tracking[12] in AI-integrated VR/AR cybersecurity training offer powerful tools for evaluating learner progress and optimizing training outcomes. AI-powered scoring and evaluation metrics can provide instant, objective assessments of a trainee's performance in various scenarios. This system can analyze multiple factors simultaneously, such as the speed of threat detection, accuracy of response, adherence to protocols, and decision-making processes. Consequently, automating this assessment, AI can provide consistent, unbiased evaluations across large numbers of trainees. The aforementioned is something that would be time-consuming and potentially inconsistent if done manually.

---

[11] Gonzalez, Avelino J., and Lorie Ramos Ingraham. "Automated exercise progression in simulation-based training." *IEEE transactions on systems, man, and cybernetics* 24.6 (1994): 863–874.

[12] Gleason, Augustus, et al. "Developing basic robotic skills using virtual reality simulation and automated assessment tools: a multidisciplinary robotic virtual reality-based curriculum using the Da Vinci Skills Simulator and tracking progress with the Intuitive Learning platform." *Journal of Robotic Surgery* 16.6 (2022): 1313–1319.

5.2 AI-Driven Enhancements in VR and AR Training

Detailed analytics on learner behavior and decision-making offer deep insights into how trainees approach cybersecurity challenges.[13] These analytics can track patterns in how learners navigate virtual environments, interact with simulated threats, and respond to various scenarios. The data collected might include eye-tracking information in VR to see what learners focus on, time spent on different tasks, the sequence of actions taken in response to threats, and even physiological responses like increased heart rate during high-stress scenarios. This wealth of data can help identify common misconceptions, areas where learners consistently struggle, and effective strategies that lead to successful outcomes.

Predictive models for skill development and knowledge retention leverage AI's capabilities to forecast a learner's future performance and areas of potential weakness. By analyzing historical performance data and comparing it with patterns from other learners, these models can predict how well a trainee is likely to retain certain information or skills over time. This can be particularly valuable in cybersecurity, where skills need to be sharp and up-to-date. VR/AR integration allows these predictive models to be applied in highly realistic, immersive scenarios, providing a more accurate assessment of how well skills will translate to real-world situations.

It's crucial to note that this type of automated assessment and tracking involves handling sensitive information about individual performance and potentially organizational vulnerabilities identified during training. As such, robust data privacy and security measures are essential. This includes encrypting all collected data, strictly controlling access to individual performance records, and ensuring that any aggregated data used for analysis is thoroughly anonymized. Organizations must comply with relevant data protection regulations and maintain transparent policies about how training data is collected, used, and stored.

The implementation of AI-powered scoring and evaluation[14] can significantly reduce the time and resources required for assessment, saving on human capital. Trainers can focus on providing personalized guidance and addressing complex issues rather than spending time on routine evaluations. However, human oversight remains important to ensure the AI's assessments align with organizational goals and to address nuanced situations that may require human judgment. The AI system can flag unusual patterns or borderline cases for human review, making a trainer's job more efficient and focused.

Analytics for learner behavior and decision-making typically involve a wide range of data points. This might include timestamps of actions taken, sequences of choices made in scenarios, accuracy rates for different types of threats, time spent analyzing various pieces of information, and patterns of interaction with virtual objects or interfaces. In VR/AR environments, additional data like physical

---

[13] Yigit, Yagmur, et al. "Enhancing Cybersecurity Training Efficacy: A Comprehensive Analysis of Gamified Learning, Behavioral Strategies and Digital Twins." *2024 IEEE 25th International Symposium on a World of Wireless, Mobile and Multimedia Networks (WoWMoM)*. IEEE, 2024.

[14] Nazaretsky, Tanya, et al. "Teachers' trust in AI‐powered educational technology and a professional development program to improve it." *British journal of educational technology* 53.4 (2022): 914–931.

movements, gaze direction, and even vocal stress levels during simulated high-pressure situations can be captured. These comprehensive analytics can reveal insights such as common decision-making pitfalls, effective problem-solving strategies, and areas where trainees tend to fixate or overlook important details.

Integrating predictive models for skill development and knowledge retention with VR/AR in AI-powered training can create a highly adaptive and forward-looking learning environment. For example, based on a trainee's performance in VR simulations, the AI might predict that their skills in network traffic analysis are likely to decline over the next few months without reinforcement. The system could then automatically schedule refresher modules in AR, perhaps overlaying network diagrams on real hardware to reinforce concepts. Similarly, if the model predicts strong retention and application of incident response skills, it might suggest more advanced scenarios in these areas, ensuring the trainee remains challenged and engaged. This predictive capability allows for proactive, personalized long-term learning plans that evolve with the trainee's growing expertise and changing cybersecurity landscape.

5.3 Designing Effective VR and AR Cybersecurity Training Modules

This section focuses on the crucial aspects of designing effective VR and AR modules for cybersecurity training. It explores the process of identifying key learning objectives and scenarios, emphasizing the importance of aligning training goals with organizational security needs and incorporating industry-specific threat landscapes. The section delves into the delicate balance between realism and usability, addressing challenges such as device optimization, user interface design, and mitigating physical discomfort. Additionally, it examines the integration of AI-powered features, including machine learning for scenario generation, computer vision for threat recognition, and natural language understanding for user interactions. Overall, this section provides a guide to creating VR and AR training modules that are not only technologically advanced but also pedagogically sound and user-friendly, ensuring maximum effectiveness in cybersecurity education.

5.3.1 Identifying Key Learning Objectives and Scenarios

Designing effective VR and AR cybersecurity training modules using AI begins with a clear identification of key learning objectives and scenarios. This process involves mapping training goals to organizational security needs, prioritizing high-impact and high-risk situations, and incorporating industry-specific threat

5.3 Designing Effective VR and AR Cybersecurity Training Modules

landscapes. AI can play a crucial role in each of these steps, helping to create more targeted, relevant, and adaptive training experiences.

Mapping training goals to organizational security needs requires a comprehensive assessment of an organization's current security posture, vulnerabilities, and strategic objectives. Organizations can start by conducting thorough risk assessments, analyzing past security incidents, and reviewing industry benchmarks. AI can assist in this process by analyzing large volumes of security data, identifying patterns and trends that might not be immediately apparent to human analysts. For instance, AI could analyze network logs, incident reports, and employee behavior data to identify common vulnerabilities or areas where security protocols are frequently bypassed. This data-driven approach ensures that training objectives are directly aligned with the most pressing security needs of the organization.

Prioritizing high-impact and high-risk situations is crucial for maximizing the effectiveness of cybersecurity training. AI can help in this prioritization by simulating various attack scenarios and assessing their potential impact on the organization. Thus, it's important to consider factors such as the likelihood of different types of attacks, the potential financial and reputational damage, and the current level of preparedness among staff. Consequently, AI can help organizations focus their training efforts on the most critical areas. This ensures that limited training resources are used most effectively, addressing the scenarios that pose the greatest risk to the organization.

Incorporating industry-specific threat landscapes into training modules is essential for preparing employees for the types of attacks they are most likely to encounter.[15] AI can continuously analyze threat intelligence feeds, industry reports, and emerging attack trends to ensure that training scenarios remain current and relevant. This dynamic approach allows organizations to rapidly adapt their training to new threats, keeping pace with the ever-evolving cybersecurity landscape. AI can also personalize these scenarios based on an employee's role and industry, ensuring that each trainee receives the most relevant and impactful training experience.

5.3.1.1 Small, Medium, and Large Organizations

For example, a small local healthcare clinic might use AI to analyze its patient data handling practices and identify that phishing attacks targeting patient information are its most significant risk. AI could then generate VR training modules simulating various phishing scenarios specific to healthcare, such as emails impersonating insurance providers or requests for patient data from fake research institutions. The training could adapt in real-time based on how employees respond, focusing more on areas where they struggle.

---

[15] Odo, Christian. "Strengthening Cybersecurity Resilience: the Importance of Education, Training, and Risk Management." *Training, and Risk Management (March 31, 2024)* (2024).

A medium-sized financial services company might leverage AI to map its training goals to regulatory compliance requirements and common financial sector threats. The AI could prioritize scenarios involving sophisticated financial fraud attempts, ransomware attacks on transaction systems, and insider threats. It might create AR modules that overlay threat indicators on simulated financial software interfaces, teaching employees to spot anomalies in real-time.[16]

For a large multinational corporation, AI could help create a comprehensive training program that addresses diverse threats across different global regions and business units. It might analyze security incidents across the organization to identify common weaknesses and create tailored VR simulations for each department. For instance, the R&D department might face scenarios involving intellectual property theft, while the manufacturing division might train on defending against industrial espionage and supply chain attacks. The AI could continuously update these scenarios based on global threat intelligence, ensuring that employees worldwide are prepared for the latest cyber threats specific to their roles and locations.

In all these cases, AI's ability to process vast amounts of data, identify patterns, and generate realistic scenarios significantly enhances the organization's capacity to create relevant, up-to-date, and effective cybersecurity training. This approach ensures that training remains aligned with organizational needs and the evolving threat landscape, ultimately leading to a more resilient and prepared workforce.

5.3.2 Balancing Realism and Usability

Balancing realism and usability is crucial in designing effective VR and AR cybersecurity training modules. While high realism can enhance the immersive experience and transfer of skills to real-world scenarios, it must not come at the cost of usability.[17] This balance is essential to ensure that trainees can focus on learning cybersecurity concepts and practices without being hindered by technical difficulties or physical discomfort.

Optimizing graphics and performance for various devices is a key consideration in this balance.[18] High-fidelity graphics can provide a more realistic and engaging experience, but they also require more processing power and can lead to performance issues on less capable devices. AI can play a significant role in this optimization process. Machine learning algorithms can dynamically adjust graphical settings

---

[16] Kayode-Ajala, Olaolu. "Applications of Cyber Threat Intelligence (CTI) in financial institutions and challenges in its adoption." *Applied Research in Artificial Intelligence and Cloud Computing* 6.8 (2023): 1–21.

[17] Sutcliffe, Alistair G., et al. "Reflecting on the design process for virtual reality applications." *International Journal of Human–Computer Interaction* 35.2 (2019): 168–179.

[18] Tytarenko, Maksym. "Optimizing Immersion: Analyzing Graphics and Performance Considerations in Unity3D VR Development." *Asian Journal of Research in Computer Science* 16.4 (2023): 104–114.

5.3 Designing Effective VR and AR Cybersecurity Training Modules

based on the user's device capabilities and performance metrics, ensuring a smooth experience across a range of hardware. For instance, AI could automatically lower texture resolution or simplify complex 3D models when it detects frame rate drops, maintaining a consistent and comfortable user experience without manual adjustments.

Designing intuitive user interfaces and controls is paramount for effective VR and AR training modules.[19] The interface should be easy to navigate and interact with, allowing users to focus on the training content rather than struggling with controls. AI can assist in creating adaptive interfaces that learn from user interactions and adjust accordingly. For example, an AI system could analyze how different users interact with the VR environment and automatically adjust the placement of virtual controls or information displays to optimize accessibility and ease of use. This personalized approach can significantly enhance the learning experience and reduce the cognitive load associated with navigating complex virtual environments.

Mitigating motion sickness and user discomfort is a critical aspect of VR and AR design, particularly for extended training sessions.[20] AI can play a crucial role in identifying and mitigating factors that contribute to discomfort. Therefore, analyzing user data such as head movements, eye tracking, and physiological responses, AI algorithms can detect early signs of motion sickness or discomfort. The system could then make real-time adjustments to the VR experience, such as reducing movement speed, adjusting the field of view, or suggesting breaks. Additionally, AI can help in personalizing comfort settings for individual users based on their past experiences and preferences. When implementing VR and AR training modules, it's important to conduct thorough testing for motion sickness and user comfort. This can involve using AI-powered analytics to gather data from test users, identifying patterns that lead to discomfort, and making iterative improvements. Organizations should look out for symptoms like dizziness, nausea, or eye strain among users and use this feedback to refine the VR/AR experience.

In order to make the training intuitive and optimized, designers should focus on creating clear, consistent interfaces that mimic real-world interactions where possible. For cybersecurity training, this might involve creating virtual replicas of common security tools and interfaces, allowing trainees to develop muscle memory that translates to real-world scenarios. AI can assist by analyzing user interactions and identifying areas where users frequently make mistakes or hesitate, suggesting improvements to make these interactions more intuitive.

Below are examples of strategies that can be utilized to minimize motion sickness and overall discomfort.

---

[19] Sutcliffe, Alistair. *Multimedia and virtual reality: designing multisensory user interfaces.* Psychology Press, 2003.

[20] Somrak, Andrej, et al. "Estimating VR Sickness and user experience using different HMD technologies: An evaluation study." *Future Generation Computer Systems* 94 (2019): 302–316.

1. Implement comfortable locomotion options, such as teleportation or snap turning, which are less likely to cause disorientation.[21]
2. Use AI to monitor and adjust the visual flow and movement speed based on individual user tolerance.[22]
3. Incorporate frequent rest points or break reminders within the training modules.
4. Utilize foveated rendering, where AI tracks eye movement to render only the focused area in high detail, reducing overall processing load and potential for discomfort.[23]

Overall, carefully balancing realism and usability, and leveraging AI to optimize the experience, organizations can create VR and AR cybersecurity training modules that are both highly effective and comfortable to use. This approach ensures that trainees can fully engage with the content, maximizing learning outcomes and skill development in a safe and controlled virtual environment.

5.3.3 Integrating AI-Powered Features and Functionalities

Integrating AI-powered features and functionalities into VR and AR cybersecurity training modules can significantly enhance the learning experience and effectiveness of the training. By leveraging machine learning for scenario generation, utilizing computer vision for object and threat recognition, and incorporating natural language understanding for user interactions, these modules can provide a more dynamic, responsive, and realistic training environment.

Implementing machine learning for scenario generation allows for the creation of highly adaptive and diverse training experiences. AI algorithms can analyze vast amounts of cybersecurity data, including real-world incident reports, threat intelligence feeds, and emerging attack patterns, to generate realistic and relevant scenarios. These scenarios can dynamically evolve based on the trainee's actions and performance, ensuring that each training session is unique and tailored to the individual's skill level and learning needs. For example, a machine learning algorithm could create a scenario simulating a sophisticated phishing attack on a financial institution. As the trainee progresses through the scenario, the AI could adjust the complexity of the attack, introducing new elements like social engineering tactics or malware variants based on the trainee's responses, constantly challenging their skills and decision-making abilities.

---

[21] Caputo, Ariel, Massimo Zancanaro, and Andrea Giachetti. "Eyes on teleporting: comparing locomotion techniques in Virtual Reality with respect to presence, sickness and spatial orientation." *IFIP Conference on Human-Computer Interaction*. Cham: Springer Nature Switzerland, 2023.

[22] Mazloumi Gavgani, Alireza, Deborah M. Hodgson, and Eugene Nalivaiko. "Effects of visual flow direction on signs and symptoms of cybersickness." *PloS one* 12.8 (2017): e0182790.

[23] Albert, Rachel, et al. "Latency requirements for foveated rendering in virtual reality." *ACM Transactions on Applied Perception (TAP)* 14.4 (2017): 1–13.

5.3 Designing Effective VR and AR Cybersecurity Training Modules

Utilizing computer vision for object and threat recognition in VR and AR environments can enhance the realism and interactivity of training modules. AI-powered computer vision can enable trainees to interact with virtual objects in a more natural and intuitive way, identifying potential threats or vulnerabilities within the simulated environment.[24] For instance, in an AR-based physical security training module, computer vision could be used to scan a real office environment and overlay virtual indicators of security risks, such as unsecured devices or potential entry points for intruders. Trainees could then practice identifying and addressing these risks in a real-world context, with the AI providing real-time feedback and guidance.

Incorporating natural language understanding for user interactions can make the training experience more immersive and accessible. This technology allows trainees to communicate with virtual assistants or simulated characters using natural language, making the training feel more realistic and engaging. For example, in a VR simulation of a SOC, trainees could use voice commands to interact with virtual systems, request information, or coordinate responses to cyber incidents. The AI could interpret these commands, provide relevant information, and even simulate conversations with team members or stakeholders, helping trainees develop their communication and leadership skills in addition to technical abilities.

For instance, imagine a VR training module for incident response. The AI generates a scenario where a healthcare organization is under a ransomware attack. As the trainee works through the incident, the AI adapts the scenario in real-time. If the trainee quickly isolates infected systems, the AI might escalate the situation by simulating a simultaneous DDoS attack, forcing the trainee to prioritize and manage multiple threats simultaneously. In an AR training module for network security, trainees wear AR glasses while examining a physical server room. The AI uses computer vision to identify network devices and overlays information about their configuration and security status. When the trainee looks at a particular switch, the AR display highlights potential vulnerabilities, such as open ports or outdated firmware, prompting the trainee to take appropriate action.

A VR simulation of a cybersecurity crisis management scenario allows trainees to interact with virtual team members and stakeholders using natural language. The trainee, acting as the Chief Information Security Officer, must brief the board of directors on a data breach. They can ask questions like, "What's the extent of the data compromised?" or "How long until we can restore operations?" The AI interprets these questions, provides relevant information, and simulates realistic responses from board members, helping the trainee practice clear communication under pressure.

---

[24] Xi, Bowei. "Adversarial machine learning for cybersecurity and computer vision: Current developments and challenges." *Wiley Interdisciplinary Reviews: Computational Statistics* 12.5 (2020): e1511.

5.4 Security Risks of VR and AR in Training Environments

This section addresses the critical issue of security risks inherent in VR and AR training environments for cybersecurity. It examines the vulnerabilities present in VR and AR hardware, highlighting real-world incidents such as the Meta VR headset hack to illustrate potential threats. The section explores data privacy and security concerns unique to these immersive technologies, including the protection of sensitive user data and compliance with data protection regulations. Additionally, it outlines strategies for mitigating these risks in cybersecurity training contexts, emphasizing the importance of robust security measures, regular audits, and user education. By thoroughly examining these security challenges, this section underscores the necessity of maintaining vigilance and implementing comprehensive safeguards in VR and AR training environments, ensuring that the tools used to teach cybersecurity do not themselves become vectors for cyber threats.

5.4.1 Vulnerabilities in VR and AR Hardware

When devices are added within an IT infrastructure, it is important to understand the risks and vulnerabilities they can introduce within an overarching security architecture. That being said, no technology is immune from being compromised by nefarious actors (or security researchers in this case). Researcher Harish Santhanalakshmi Ganesan, who successfully installed malware on Meta's Quest 3 VR headset without enabling developer mode, demonstrated how VR could be compromised.[25] Ganesan's approach exploited the fact that Meta's Quest 3 uses a restricted version of the Android Open Source Project (AOSP), which allowed him to install APK files similar to installing apps on an Android phone. Using an app from Meta's App Lab that provides access to Android's native file manager, Ganesan was able to install CovidLock ransomware on the headset. While CovidLock was used in this demonstration, Ganesan emphasized that this method could potentially be used to deliver any type of malware.

The significance of this case study lies in its revelation of a new attack surface in VR technology. It demonstrates that VR headsets, despite their specialized nature, can be vulnerable to malware attacks traditionally associated with smartphones and computers. This discovery has far-reaching implications for the future of VR technology, especially in sensitive applications like AI-powered cybersecurity training.

---

[25] Meta's Virtual Reality Headset Vulnerable to Ransomware Attacks: Researcher. 2024, June 25th. Security Week. https://www.securityweek.com/metas-virtual-reality-headset-vulnerable-to-ransomware-attacks-researcher/#:~:text=Ransomware-,Meta's%20Virtual%20Reality%20Headset%20Vulnerable%20to%20Ransomware%20Attacks%3A%20Researcher,Meta's%20Quest%203%20VR%20headset.&text=Spatial%20computing%20attacks%20targeting%20VR%20headsets%20are%20rare.

5.4 Security Risks of VR and AR in Training Environments

It highlights the need for robust security measures in VR systems, particularly as they become more prevalent in professional and educational settings.

Looking to the future, this vulnerability could have significant consequences. As VR and AR technologies become more integrated into various sectors, including cybersecurity training, the potential for malicious exploitation grows. Attackers could potentially use similar methods to compromise VR-based training environments, injecting malware that could disrupt training sessions, steal sensitive data, or even manipulate the training content itself. This could lead to misinformed or poorly trained cybersecurity professionals, ultimately weakening an organization's security posture. The potential exploitation of sensors and input devices in VR and AR hardware presents another layer of concern. These devices often include sophisticated sensors for tracking movement, eye gaze, and even biometric data. In the context of AI-powered cybersecurity training, compromised sensors could lead to data breaches of highly sensitive information. For instance, eye-tracking data[26] could reveal which parts of a security interface a trainee focuses on, potentially exposing vulnerabilities in an organization's security protocols. Organizations implementing AI-powered cyber training in VR/AR must be acutely aware of these hardware vulnerabilities and implement stringent security measures to protect both the training environment and the data it generates.

Risks associated with wireless connectivity in VR/AR systems add another dimension to these security challenges. Many VR and AR devices rely on wireless connections for data transmission, updates, and interaction with other systems. This wireless functionality, while convenient, opens up potential avenues for attack. In an AI-powered training scenario, a compromised wireless connection could allow attackers to intercept training data, inject malicious content into simulations, or even gain unauthorized access to the broader network infrastructure supporting the training environment. The importance of considering these risks cannot be overstated. As organizations increasingly adopt VR and AR for AI-powered cybersecurity training, they must recognize that these platforms introduce new and unique security challenges. The immersive nature of VR/AR, combined with the sensitive nature of cybersecurity training, creates a potent mix of valuable data and potential vulnerabilities. Organizations must implement comprehensive security strategies that address not only the software aspects of these systems but also the hardware and connectivity components. This may include regular security audits of VR/AR hardware, strict protocols for wireless connectivity, and ongoing monitoring for unusual activities or data flows within these systems.

---

[26] Blascheck, Tanja, et al. "Visualization of eye tracking data: A taxonomy and survey." *Computer Graphics Forum*. Vol. 36. No. 8. 2017.

5.4.2 Data Privacy and Security Concerns

In the context of AR/VR and AI-powered cybersecurity training, data privacy and security concerns are paramount. The integration of these technologies introduces new challenges in protecting sensitive user information, particularly biometric and behavioral data. VR and AR systems often collect vast amounts of data, including eye movements, facial expressions, and body language, which can be highly revealing about an individual's cognitive processes and emotional states.[27] In cybersecurity training scenarios, this data could potentially expose vulnerabilities in an organization's security practices or reveal individual weaknesses that could be exploited.

To address these concerns, organizations implementing AR/VR and AI-powered cybersecurity training should adopt a data minimization approach.[28] This involves carefully considering what data is absolutely necessary for the training process and avoiding the capture and storage of extraneous information. For example, while tracking a trainee's eye movements might be crucial for assessing their attention to detail in identifying security threats, storing long-term records of this data may not be necessary. Organizations should implement systems that process this data in real-time for immediate feedback but avoid long-term storage of raw biometric data.

The regulatory landscape surrounding data privacy and AI is rapidly evolving, with laws like the EU AI Act, Colorado AI Act, and various state-level data privacy and minimization laws coming into effect. These regulations often classify AI systems used in educational settings as high-risk, requiring stringent compliance measures. To navigate this complex regulatory environment, organizations should implement robust data governance policies that clearly define what data is collected, how it's used, and how long it's retained. In some instances, this data will not even be allowed to be collected. Thus, organizations need to clearly understand what laws are applicable tot hem and how they can comply with them. Consulting with legal experts will be crucial. While this can disproportionately affect smaller organizations, as they often lack the resources and capital to have these experts in house or on retainer, compliance with legal requirements is of the utmost importance. They should also ensure transparent communication with trainees about data collection practices and obtain explicit consent for any data processing activities.

When determining what data to store, organizations should focus on aggregated, anonymized metrics that provide insights into training effectiveness without compromising individual privacy. For instance, instead of storing detailed records of a trainee's performance in specific scenarios, the system could retain overall scores or

---

[27] Roesner, Franziska, and Tadayoshi Kohno. "Security and privacy for augmented reality: Our 10-year retrospective." *VR4Sec: 1st International Workshop on Security for XR and XR for Security.* 2021.

[28] Biega, Asia J., et al. "Operationalizing the legal principle of data minimization for personalization." *Proceedings of the 43rd international ACM SIGIR conference on research and development in information retrieval.* 2020.

5.4 Security Risks of VR and AR in Training Environments

general areas of improvement. Hypothetically, a VR-based phishing detection training module might track success rates in identifying various types of phishing attempts, but it shouldn't store the specific actions or mistakes made by individual trainees.

Securing communication between VR/AR devices and servers is crucial to protect both the integrity of the training process and the confidentiality of user data. Organizations should implement end-to-end encryption for all data transmissions between devices and servers. This includes using strong, up-to-date encryption protocols and ensuring that encryption keys are properly managed and rotated regularly. Additionally, implementing secure authentication mechanisms, such as multi-factor authentication, for both devices and users can help prevent unauthorized access to training systems and data.

Another important step in securing VR/AR communications is the use of virtual private networks (VPNs) or dedicated secure channels for data transmission.[29] This can help protect against man-in-the-middle attacks and ensure that training data remains confidential even if intercepted. Regular security audits and penetration testing of the communication infrastructure can help identify and address potential vulnerabilities before they can be exploited.

As a hypothetical example, consider an organization using a VR-based incident response training system. The system simulates a complex cyber attack, and trainees must navigate through various scenarios to contain and mitigate the threat. To secure this training environment, the organization could implement a multitude of measures. Securing a VR-based incident response training system will require a multi-faceted approach. Organizations should implement a comprehensive set of measures. These include using end-to-end encryption for all data transmitted between VR headsets and the central training server, and setting up a secure, dedicated network for the training environment that is isolated from the organization's main network. Multi-factor authentication should be employed for trainees accessing the system, combining knowledge factors (like passwords), possession factors (such as security tokens), and potentially biometric verification. To minimize data exposure, trainee performance data should be processed and analyzed in real-time on the VR device itself, with only aggregated, anonymized results transmitted to the central server for long-term storage and analysis. Finally, regular security audits and penetration testing should be conducted to identify and address potential vulnerabilities, ensuring the ongoing robustness of the system's security measures. These steps collectively create a secure training environment that protects sensitive data while leveraging the benefits of VR and AI for cybersecurity training.

---

[29] Wang, Su. "Application Research of MPLS VPN and VR Panoramic Technology in Virtual Network of Party School System." *Proceedings of the 2020 International Conference on Computers, Information Processing and Advanced Education.* 2020.

5.4.3 Mitigating Risks in VR and AR Cybersecurity Training

Mitigating risks in VR and AR cybersecurity training requires a multi-faceted approach, starting with implementing robust authentication and encryption measures. Traditional encryption methods may become vulnerable to quantum computing attacks in the future, making it crucial to consider post-quantum cryptography (PQC) in the design of VR/AR training systems. Organizations should begin transitioning to quantum-resistant algorithms for data encryption and key exchange protocols.[30] This proactive approach ensures that sensitive training data remains secure even as quantum computing technology advances. Additionally, multi-factor authentication should be standard practice, combining biometric data (like retinal scans or hand gestures unique to VR interactions), hardware tokens, and knowledge-based factors to ensure only authorized personnel can access the training environments.

Regular security audits and vulnerability assessments are essential for maintaining the integrity of VR/AR cybersecurity training systems. For small organizations, this might involve quarterly internal reviews combined with annual third-party assessments. Medium-sized organizations should consider more frequent external audits, perhaps bi-annually, along with continuous internal monitoring. Large organizations with complex VR/AR training infrastructures should implement continuous monitoring and assessment protocols, potentially using AI-driven tools to detect anomalies in real-time. These audits should cover not only the software components but also the hardware devices, focusing on firmware vulnerabilities, sensor data security, and potential exploits in the VR/AR operating systems.

Educating users on safe VR/AR practices and potential threats is crucial for maintaining the security of these training environments. Users need to be aware of the unique risks associated with VR/AR technologies, such as the potential for malware to exploit immersive environments to collect sensitive data or manipulate user perceptions. They should be trained to recognize signs of compromised systems, such as unexpected visual artifacts or unusual system behaviors. Users also need to understand the importance of physical security when using VR/AR devices, ensuring that their surrounding environment is secure to prevent real-world threats during immersive training sessions.

Creating an effective education program for disseminating knowledge about safe VR/AR practices and potential threats is key. Kind of seems like a circle, doesn't it? Organizations should develop a comprehensive curriculum that covers both general cybersecurity principles and VR/AR-specific threats. This program could include interactive VR/AR modules that simulate potential security threats, allowing users to practice identifying and responding to them in a safe environment. Regular workshops or webinars should be conducted to update users on the latest VR/AR security trends and emerging threats. Gamified learning experiences can be incorporated to

---

[30] Campbell, Robert, Whitfield Diffie, and Charles Robinson. "Advancements in Quantum Computing and AI May Impact PQC Migration Timelines." (2024).

reward users for demonstrating good security practices in VR/AR environments, making the learning process more engaging and memorable. Collaborative exercises should be included to encourage users to share experiences and best practices with their peers, fostering a culture of security awareness. Finally, periodic assessments should be implemented to ensure users retain and apply the knowledge gained from the training program, helping to reinforce the importance of ongoing vigilance in VR/AR security practices. The key is to maintain a balance between leveraging the full potential of VR/AR technologies for effective training and implementing stringent security measures to protect against evolving cyber threats.

5.5 Future Trends and Innovations in VR/AR Cybersecurity Training

This section explores the exciting frontier of VR and AR in cybersecurity training, focusing on future trends and innovations that promise to revolutionize the field. It examines the potential integration of VR and AR with other emerging technologies such as IoT and 5G, and even speculates on the role of brain-computer interfaces in training. The section delves into anticipated advancements in AI-driven scenarios, including more sophisticated AI agents and dynamically generated training environments. Additionally, it addresses current limitations and challenges in VR/AR training, discussing potential solutions to hardware constraints, haptic feedback realism, and the need for standardized effectiveness measures. Overall, this section provides insight into the evolving landscape of VR and AR in cybersecurity education, highlighting the continuous innovation driving this field toward more immersive, effective, and accessible training experiences.

5.5.1 Integration with Other Emerging Technologies

The integration of VR/AR with other emerging technologies, alongside AI, presents a groundbreaking opportunity for organizations to revolutionize their cybersecurity training programs. Interestingly, combining VR/AR with Internet of Things (IoT) devices, organizations can create highly realistic physical security training scenarios.[31] For instance, trainees could navigate virtual environments where they interact with simulated IoT devices, learning to identify and mitigate security vulnerabilities in smart buildings or industrial control systems. AI could dynamically adjust these scenarios, introducing new threats based on real-world data from IoT networks.

---

[31] Ficco, Massimo, and Francesco Palmieri. "Leaf: An open-source cybersecurity training platform for realistic edge-IoT scenarios." *Journal of Systems Architecture* 97 (2019): 107–129.

Leveraging 5G technology in conjunction with VR/AR and AI for cybersecurity training offers transformative possibilities. The ultra-low latency and high bandwidth of 5G networks can dramatically reduce the lag between user actions and system responses in VR/AR environments, creating a more immersive and realistic experience.[32] This enhanced responsiveness is crucial for cybersecurity training, where split-second decisions can be critical. With 5G, complex simulations involving multiple interconnected systems and large amounts of data can be rendered and updated in real-time, allowing for more sophisticated and dynamic training scenarios.

The high-speed capabilities of 5G also enable seamless collaboration between multiple trainees in shared virtual environments, regardless of their physical locations. This opens up possibilities for large-scale, distributed training exercises that were previously impractical due to network limitations. For instance, organizations could simulate coordinated cyber attacks across geographically dispersed infrastructure, with trainees from different locations working together in a shared virtual space to detect, respond to, and mitigate these threats. Such exercises can help prepare cybersecurity teams for the complexities of real-world, large-scale incidents that require coordinated responses across multiple departments or even organizations.

The integration of brain-computer interfaces (BCIs) with VR/AR and AI in cybersecurity training represents a frontier in human-computer interaction.[33] BCIs could potentially allow trainees to interact with virtual environments and simulated systems using neural signals, providing a more intuitive and rapid means of control. This could be particularly valuable in high-stress scenarios where quick reactions are crucial. For example, a trainee might be able to activate certain security protocols or navigate through complex system interfaces simply by thinking about the action, rather than using traditional input methods. The integration of BCIs in cybersecurity training, coupled with AI analysis, offers unprecedented insights into the cognitive processes of cybersecurity professionals. AI algorithms could analyze brain activity data in real-time, assessing various critical factors that influence performance and learning. By monitoring neural indicators of stress, trainers could identify particularly challenging scenarios or tasks, enabling more targeted skill development. Understanding the cognitive load imposed by different tasks could inform the design of more effective training programs and help optimize real-world workflows to reduce mental fatigue. Additionally, analysis of brain activity during critical decision points could reveal patterns in how successful cybersecurity professionals approach complex problems, potentially shaping best practices and training methodologies.

Furthermore, BCIs could help identify fluctuations in attention and focus, allowing for dynamic adjustments to training difficulty or the introduction of new

---

[32] Hamza, Muhammad Ali, Usama Ejaz, and Hyun-chul Kim. "Cyber5Gym: An Integrated Framework for 5G Cybersecurity Training." *Electronics* 13.5 (2024): 888.

[33] Nicolas-Alonso, Luis Fernando, and Jaime Gomez-Gil. "Brain computer interfaces, a review." *sensors* 12.2 (2012): 1211–1279.

5.5 Future Trends and Innovations in VR/AR Cybersecurity Training

challenges to maintain optimal engagement.[34] Understanding the emotional states of trainees during various scenarios could also contribute to developing strategies for maintaining composure and effectiveness under pressure. This level of detailed cognitive insight could revolutionize cybersecurity training, allowing for highly personalized programs tailored to individual learning styles and cognitive strengths. It could also inform the development of more effective team compositions by matching professionals with complementary cognitive profiles for optimal performance in high-stakes situations.

This level of insight into the cognitive aspects of cybersecurity work could lead to highly personalized training programs, tailored to individual learning styles and cognitive strengths. It could also contribute to the development of more effective team compositions, matching professionals with complementary cognitive profiles for optimal performance in high-stakes situations. However, the integration of BCIs also raises significant ethical and privacy concerns. The collection and analysis of neural data is a sensitive issue that requires careful consideration of data protection, informed consent, and potential misuse. Organizations would need to establish robust protocols for handling this data and ensure that trainees fully understand and consent to its collection and use.

Organizations that successfully integrate these technologies could set themselves apart by offering unparalleled, cutting-edge training experiences. The benefits include more effective skill development, better retention of knowledge through highly engaging and realistic simulations, and the ability to rapidly adapt training content to emerging threats. Moreover, this integrated approach could lead to more accurate assessments of cybersecurity readiness and help identify areas for improvement at both individual and organizational levels.

However, the drawbacks and security challenges of integrating these technologies are significant. First off, there may be huge reluctance to adopt the aforementioned on both the employee and organizational front. Each additional technology introduces new vulnerabilities and attack surfaces. For example, IoT devices are notorious for their security weaknesses, and integrating them into training systems could potentially expose sensitive data. The use of BCIs raises very serious privacy concerns regarding the collection and protection of neural data. 5G networks, while offering enhanced capabilities, also introduce new security considerations related to network slicing and edge computing.

Resource constraints pose a major challenge, as implementing and maintaining such advanced systems requires significant investment in hardware, software, and expertise. Many organizations may lack the necessary understanding of these technologies to implement them effectively and securely. The shortage of human capital with expertise in these cutting-edge fields further complicates matters. It's crucial for organizations to stay abreast of security best practices for all involved technologies, which can be a daunting task given the rapid pace of technological advancement.

---

[34] He, Bin, et al. "Brain–computer interfaces." *Neural engineering* (2020): 131–183.

A hypothetical scenario illustrating the integration of these technologies might involve a large financial institution creating a comprehensive cybersecurity training program. Trainees would wear VR headsets equipped with BCIs, entering a virtual representation of the bank's headquarters. IoT sensors throughout the physical office would feed real-time data into the simulation, creating a dynamic environment that mirrors the actual state of the building's systems. 5G connectivity would enable multiple trainees to interact simultaneously in this virtual space, responding to a simulated cyber attack orchestrated by AI.

In this scenario, the AI might simulate a multi-vector attack involving a phishing campaign, malware infection, and attempted physical breach. Trainees would need to collaborate to identify and respond to these threats, with the BCI tracking their stress levels and decision-making processes. The IoT integration would allow trainees to interact with virtual representations of real security systems, practicing both cybersecurity and physical security protocols. The high-speed, low-latency 5G network would ensure that all these elements work together seamlessly, providing a highly realistic and responsive training environment. While this scenario demonstrates the potential for revolutionary training experiences, it also highlights the complexity and potential vulnerabilities of such an integrated system. Organizations pursuing this level of technological integration must be prepared to invest heavily in security measures, regular audits, and ongoing training for both users and administrators of these systems. The potential benefits in terms of enhanced preparedness and skill development must be carefully weighed against the increased risk surface and resource requirements.

5.5.2 Advancements in AI-Driven VR/AR Training Scenarios

Advancements in AI-driven VR/AR training scenarios are poised to revolutionize cybersecurity education by creating more immersive, challenging, and realistic training environments. One of the key areas of development is in creating more sophisticated AI opponents and allies. By leveraging game theory, AI systems can be designed to make strategic decisions that more closely mimic human behavior, both in adversarial and collaborative roles. Game theory provides a framework for understanding and predicting decision-making in competitive and cooperative situations, which is highly relevant in cybersecurity contexts.

For instance, an AI opponent in a training scenario could use game theoretical principles to make decisions about when and how to launch attacks, considering factors like risk, reward, and the trainee's likely responses. This approach could lead to more unpredictable and realistic attack patterns, forcing trainees to think critically and adapt their strategies in real-time. Similarly, AI allies could use game theory to make more nuanced decisions about resource allocation and information sharing, simulating the complexities of real-world team dynamics in cybersecurity operations.

The development of dynamically generated, infinite training scenarios[35] represents another significant advancement in AI-driven VR/AR training. Traditional training scenarios are often limited and can become predictable over time. However, with advanced AI algorithms, it's possible to create scenarios that are unique each time a trainee enters the virtual environment. These algorithms can consider various factors such as the trainee's skill level, past performance, specific learning objectives, and current cybersecurity trends to generate tailored, relevant scenarios on the fly.

This capability for infinite scenario generation ensures that training remains challenging and engaging, even for experienced professionals. It allows for continuous learning and adaptation, mirroring the ever-changing landscape of cybersecurity threats. Moreover, it can help prevent the development of routine responses, encouraging trainees to remain vigilant and think creatively in each new situation they encounter.

Improving the emotional intelligence of AI-driven virtual characters is another crucial aspect of advancing VR/AR training scenarios. In real-world cybersecurity situations, professionals often need to interact with colleagues, stakeholders, and even adversaries, requiring not just technical skills but also emotional intelligence and communication abilities. By enhancing the emotional responses and interactive capabilities of virtual characters, training scenarios can better prepare cybersecurity professionals for the human aspects of their work.

AI models can be developed to exhibit more nuanced emotional responses, body language, and conversational patterns. This could include simulating stressed colleagues during a cyber attack, portraying the anxiety of executives during a data breach, or mimicking the subtle cues of social engineering attempts. By interacting with these emotionally intelligent virtual characters, trainees can develop better communication skills, learn to manage high-stress situations, and improve their ability to detect and respond to social engineering tactics.

The combination of these advancements—sophisticated AI opponents and allies, dynamically generated scenarios, and emotionally intelligent virtual characters—creates a powerful ecosystem for cybersecurity training. This ecosystem can adapt to the individual needs of each trainee, providing personalized learning experiences that are both challenging and relevant. It can simulate a wide range of situations, from routine security operations to complex, multi-faceted cyber-attacks, allowing professionals to gain experience in a safe, controlled environment.

However, as highlighted throughout this book, implementing these advanced AI-driven scenarios also presents challenges. It requires significant computational resources and expertise to develop and maintain such sophisticated systems. There's also the risk of AI biases being introduced into the training scenarios, which could lead to skewed learning outcomes. Therefore, it's crucial to have robust testing and

---

[35] Perez-Liebana, Diego, et al. "General video game ai: A multitrack framework for evaluating agents, games, and content generation algorithms." *IEEE Transactions on Games* 11.3 (2019): 195–214.

validation processes in place to ensure the AI models are fair, accurate, and aligned with real-world cybersecurity practices.

Hypotehtical scenario time! How can small and medium sized entities (SMEs) and large organizations adopt the aforementioned? Let's start with a small organization, a local credit union. A local credit union with 50 employees implements an AI-driven VR training program to enhance their cybersecurity preparedness. They use a cloud-based platform that offers dynamically generated scenarios tailored to financial institutions. Employees utilize VR headsets to enter a virtual replica of their credit union. The AI generates unique phishing attempts and social engineering scenarios based on current trends in financial sector attacks. Emotionally intelligent virtual characters simulate members requesting sensitive information, testing employees' ability to follow security protocols while maintaining customer service. The system uses game theory to create AI opponents that adapt their strategies based on employee responses, simulating increasingly sophisticated attack attempts. This approach helps the credit union's small team develop a broad range of skills without the need for extensive in-house IT resources.

Moving on to a medium sized organization, like a regional hospital, could also benefit from advancements in AI powered cybersecurity training with the use of AR/VR. Let's say a regional hospital implements an advanced AI-driven VR/AR training system to improve its cybersecurity and HIPAA compliance. The hospital creates a virtual twin of its facility, including patient rooms, nurses' stations, and IT infrastructure. Training scenarios dynamically generate situations involving patient data breaches, ransomware attacks on medical devices, and social engineering attempts targeting staff. AI-driven virtual characters simulate patients, visitors, and staff with varying emotional states, helping healthcare professionals practice maintaining data security in high-stress situations. The system uses game theory to create complex, multi-vector attack scenarios that evolve based on the trainees' actions, testing the hospital's incident response capabilities across different departments.

Now let's imagine a large organization, a multinational tech corporation with a state-of-the-art AI-driven VR/AR cybersecurity training program. The company creates a vast virtual environment simulating its global operations, including offices, data centers, and manufacturing facilities. The AI generates infinite, interconnected scenarios that mirror the company's complex digital ecosystem. Trainees from different departments and geographical locations collaborate in shared virtual spaces to respond to sophisticated cyber attacks. AI opponents, developed using advanced game theory models, simulate nation-state level threats and corporate espionage attempts, adapting their strategies in real-time based on the company's defenses.

The system incorporates emotionally intelligent virtual characters representing employees, executives, and external stakeholders from various cultural backgrounds. This helps train staff in managing the human aspects of global cybersecurity incidents, including crisis communication and cross-cultural collaboration. The AI continuously analyzes global threat intelligence and the company's own security data to generate relevant, up-to-date scenarios. It also provides personalized training paths for each employee based on their role, skill level, and performance history.

In all three cases, the organizations benefit from tailored, realistic training experiences that adapt to their specific needs and scale. The small credit union gains access to sophisticated training without extensive resources, the hospital improves its ability to protect sensitive patient data, and the large corporation enhances its global security posture through complex, collaborative scenarios. Each implementation demonstrates how AI-driven VR/AR training can be scaled and customized to meet the unique cybersecurity challenges of organizations of different sizes and industries.

5.5.3   *Overcoming Current Limitations and Challenges*

Overcoming current limitations and challenges in VR/AR cybersecurity training is crucial for the widespread adoption and effectiveness of these technologies. One significant hurdle is addressing hardware constraints and accessibility issues. While VR and AR technologies have advanced significantly, high-quality headsets and supporting hardware can still be expensive and may require powerful computing resources. This can limit accessibility, especially for smaller organizations or individual learners. AI can play a role in mitigating these issues by optimizing content delivery and performance. For instance, AI algorithms can dynamically adjust the complexity of virtual environments based on the available hardware, ensuring a smooth experience even on less powerful devices. Additionally, AI can help in developing more efficient rendering techniques, potentially reducing the hardware requirements for immersive experiences.

Enhancing the realism of haptic feedback[36] in VR training presents another challenge. Current haptic technologies often fall short in providing truly realistic sensations, which can break immersion and limit the effectiveness of certain training scenarios. AI can contribute to improving haptic feedback by analyzing real-world tactile interactions and generating more accurate and nuanced haptic responses in virtual environments. Machine learning models could be trained on vast datasets of physical interactions to create more lifelike haptic simulations. However, the integration of advanced haptic systems with AI also introduces new complexities in terms of data processing and real-time response, potentially requiring more sophisticated hardware.

Developing standards for VR/AR cybersecurity training effectiveness is essential for ensuring that these new training methodologies deliver measurable and consistent results. AI can be instrumental in creating and implementing these standards. For example, AI-driven analytics can be used to assess trainee performance across various scenarios, providing objective metrics for skill development and knowledge retention. These analytics can help in establishing benchmarks and identifying best

---

[36] MacLean, Karon E. "Designing with haptic feedback." *Proceedings 2000 ICRA. Millennium conference. IEEE international conference on robotics and automation. Symposia proceedings (cat. no. 00ch37065)*. Vol. 1. IEEE, 2000.

practices in VR/AR training. AI can also assist in continuously evaluating and refining training modules based on aggregate performance data, ensuring that the training remains effective and relevant as cybersecurity threats evolve.

However, the use of AI in developing these standards also presents challenges. There's a risk of bias in AI algorithms, which could lead to skewed assessments or standards that don't accurately reflect the diverse needs of different organizations or individuals. Additionally, as AI becomes more integral to training systems, there's a need to ensure that the AI itself is secure and not vulnerable to manipulation, which could compromise the integrity of the training programs.

Addressing these challenges requires a collaborative effort between VR/AR developers, cybersecurity experts, and AI researchers. As these technologies converge, new possibilities emerge for creating more accessible, realistic, and effective training experiences. However, it's crucial to approach these advancements with a critical eye, ensuring that the integration of AI enhances rather than complicates the training process. By carefully navigating these challenges and leveraging the strengths of AI, the field of VR/AR cybersecurity training can continue to evolve, offering increasingly sophisticated and valuable tools for developing cybersecurity skills in an ever-changing threat landscape.

As we conclude this exploration of AI's transformative role in cybersecurity training, it becomes evident that we stand at the cusp of a new era in educational technology. The integration of artificial intelligence into cybersecurity education offers unprecedented opportunities to create more effective, engaging, and personalized learning experiences. From adaptive learning systems that cater to individual needs, to immersive simulations that replicate real-world threat scenarios, AI is revolutionizing how we prepare the next generation of cybersecurity professionals.

Throughout this book, we've examined the multifaceted applications of AI in cybersecurity training. We've seen how AI-driven personalized learning can address individual knowledge gaps and enhance learner engagement. We've explored the power of gamification and immersive learning experiences in promoting active skill acquisition. The potential of AI to generate dynamic and evolving threat simulations has been highlighted, demonstrating its capacity to prepare learners for the ever-changing landscape of cyber threats. Furthermore, we've delved into the exciting world of AI-enhanced virtual and augmented reality, showcasing how these technologies can create highly realistic and interactive training environments.

However, as we embrace these technological advancements, we must also remain vigilant about the security risks they may introduce. The discussion on potential vulnerabilities in VR and AR systems serves as a crucial reminder that even as we use these tools to teach cybersecurity, we must apply cybersecurity principles to protect the tools themselves. This underscores the cyclical nature of cybersecurity education and practice—as we develop new technologies, we must simultaneously evolve our security measures.

Looking to the future, the potential for AI in cybersecurity training appears boundless. As AI technologies continue to advance, we can anticipate even more sophisticated, responsive, and effective training methodologies. The integration of AI with other emerging technologies, such as IoT and 5G, promises to further enhance the realism and effectiveness of cybersecurity training. However, as we progress, it will be crucial to address current limitations, establish standards for effectiveness, and ensure that these advanced training methods remain accessible to a wide range of learners.

In conclusion, the marriage of AI and cybersecurity training represents a powerful alliance in our ongoing battle against cyber threats. By leveraging AI to create more intelligent, adaptive, and immersive learning experiences, we can better equip cybersecurity professionals with the skills and knowledge they need to protect our digital world. As we move forward, it will be essential to continue innovating, adapting, and refining these AI-driven training methodologies, always keeping pace with the evolving threat landscape. The future of cybersecurity training is here, and it is powered by artificial intelligence. Thank you so much for reading and go out there and create a safer digital future!

References

1. Hue, M.-t., & Li, W.-s. (2008). *Classroom management: Creating a positive learning environment* (Vol. 1). Hong Kong University Press.
2. Wagner, P., & Alharthi, D. (2023). Leveraging VR/AR/MR/XR technologies to improve cybersecurity education, training, and operations. *Journal of Cybersecurity Education, Research and Practice, 2024*(1), 7.
3. Myneni, S. (2022). *Defeating attackers by bridging the gaps between security and intelligence.* Arizona State University.
4. Rampolla, J., & Kipper, G. (2012). *Augmented reality: An emerging technologies guide to AR.* Elsevier.
5. Smart Glasses Made Smarter with Meta AI. Meta. https://www.meta.com/smart-glasses
6. This Is Meta Quest. Meta. https://www.meta.com/quest
7. Qawasmeh, S. A.-D., AlQahtani, A. A. S., & Khan, M. K. (2024). Navigating cybersecurity training: A comprehensive review. *arXiv preprint arXiv, 2401*, 11326.
8. Churchill, E. F., Snowdon, D. N., & Munro, A. J. (Eds.). (2012). *Collaborative virtual environments: Digital places and spaces for interaction.* Springer.
9. Wang, M., et al. (2022). Intelligent virtual case learning system based on real medical records and natural language processing. *BMC Medical Informatics and Decision Making, 22*(1), 60.
10. Papakostas, C., Troussas, C., & Sgouropoulou, C. (2024). Review of the literature on AI-enhanced augmented reality in education. *Special Topics in Artificial Intelligence and Augmented Reality: The Case of Spatial Intelligence Enhancement*, 13–50.
11. Stanney, K. M., et al. (2022). Performance gains from adaptive eXtended reality training fueled by artificial intelligence. *The Journal of Defense Modeling and Simulation, 19*(2), 195–218.
12. Gonzalez, A. J., & Ingraham, L. R. (1994). Automated exercise progression in simulation-based training. *IEEE Transactions on Systems, Man, and Cybernetics, 24*(6), 863–874.
13. Gleason, A., et al. (2022). Developing basic robotic skills using virtual reality simulation and automated assessment tools: A multidisciplinary robotic virtual reality-based curriculum using the Da Vinci skills simulator and tracking progress with the intuitive learning platform. *Journal of Robotic Surgery, 16*(6), 1313–1319.
14. Yigit, Y., et al. Enhancing cybersecurity training efficacy: A comprehensive analysis of gamified learning, behavioral strategies and digital twins. In *2024 IEEE 25th international symposium on a world of wireless, Mobile and Multimedia Networks (WoWMoM)* (p. 2024). IEEE.

15. Nazaretsky, T., et al. (2022). Teachers' trust in AI-powered educational technology and a professional development program to improve it. *British Journal of Educational Technology, 53*(4), 914–931.
16. Odo, C. (2024). Strengthening cybersecurity resilience: The importance of education, training, and risk management. *Training, and Risk Management*.
17. Kayode-Ajala, O. (2023). Applications of cyber threat intelligence (CTI) in financial institutions and challenges in its adoption. *Applied Research in Artificial Intelligence and Cloud Computing, 6*(8), 1–21.
18. Sutcliffe, A. G., et al. (2019). Reflecting on the design process for virtual reality applications. *International Journal of Human–Computer Interaction, 35*(2), 168–179.
19. Tytarenko, M. (2023). Optimizing immersion: Analyzing graphics and performance considerations in Unity3D VR development. *Asian Journal of Research in Computer Science, 16*(4), 104–114.
20. Sutcliffe, A. (2003). *Multimedia and virtual reality: Designing multisensory user interfaces*. Psychology Press.
21. Somrak, A., et al. (2019). Estimating VR sickness and user experience using different HMD technologies: An evaluation study. *Future Generation Computer Systems, 94*, 302–316.
22. Caputo, A., Zancanaro, M., & Giachetti, A. (2023). Eyes on teleporting: Comparing locomotion techniques in virtual reality with respect to presence, sickness and spatial orientation. In *IFIP Conference on Human-Computer Interaction*. Springer.
23. Mazloumi Gavgani, A., Hodgson, D. M., & Nalivaiko, E. (2017). Effects of visual flow direction on signs and symptoms of cybersickness. *PLoS One, 12*(8), e0182790.
24. Albert, R., et al. (2017). Latency requirements for foveated rendering in virtual reality. *ACM Transactions on Applied Perception (TAP), 14*(4), 1–13.
25. Xi, B. (2020). Adversarial machine learning for cybersecurity and computer vision: Current developments and challenges. *Wiley Interdisciplinary Reviews: Computational Statistics, 12*(5), e1511.
26. Meta's Virtual Reality Headset Vulnerable to Ransomware Attacks: Researcher. (2024, June 25). *Security week*. https://www.securityweek.com/metas-virtual-reality-headset-vulnerable-to-ransomware-attacks-researcher/#:~:text=Ransomware-,Meta's%20Virtual%20Reality%20Headset%20Vulnerable%20to%20Ransomware%20Attacks%3A%20Researcher,Meta's%20Quest%203%20VR%20headset.&text=Spatial%20computing%20attacks%20targeting%20VR%20headsets%20are%20rare
27. Blascheck, T., et al. (2017). Visualization of eye tracking data: A taxonomy and survey. *Computer Graphics Forum, 36*(8).
28. Roesner, F., & Kohno, T. (2021). Security and privacy for augmented reality: Our 10-year retrospective. *VR4Sec: 1st International Workshop on Security for XR and XR for Security*.
29. Biega, A. J., et al. (2020). Operationalizing the legal principle of data minimization for personalization. In *Proceedings of the 43rd international ACM SIGIR conference on research and development in information retrieval*.
30. Wang, S. (2020). Application Research of MPLS VPN and VR Panoramic Technology in Virtual Network of Party School System. In *Proceedings of the 2020 International Conference on Computers, Information Processing and Advanced Education*.
31. Campbell, R., Diffie, W., & Robinson, C. (2024). *Advancements in quantum computing and AI may impact PQC migration timelines*.
32. Ficco, M., & Palmieri, F. (2019). Leaf: An open-source cybersecurity training platform for realistic edge-IoT scenarios. *Journal of Systems Architecture, 97*, 107–129.
33. Hamza, M. A., Ejaz, U., & Kim, H.-c. (2024). Cyber5Gym: An integrated framework for 5G cybersecurity training. *Electronics, 13*(5), 888.
34. Nicolas-Alonso, L. F., & Gomez-Gil, J. (2012). Brain computer interfaces, a review. *Sensors, 12*(2), 1211–1279.
35. He, B., et al. (2020). Brain–computer interfaces. *Neural Engineering*, 131–183.

36. Perez-Liebana, D., et al. (2019). General video game AI: A multitrack framework for evaluating agents, games, and content generation algorithms. *IEEE Transactions on Games, 11*(3), 195–214.
37. MacLean, K. E. (2000). Designing with haptic feedback. In *Proceedings 2000 ICRA. Millennium conference. IEEE international conference on robotics and automation. Symposia proceedings (cat. no. 00ch37065)* (Vol. 1). IEEE.